$\mathcal{U}$m, Like ✻✻✻ OM

A Girl Goddess's Guide to Yoga

Um, Like ... OM
A Girl Goddess's Guide to Yoga

BY EVAN COOPER

ILLUSTRATED BY STACY PETERSON

LITTLE, BROWN AND COMPANY

New York · Boston

Neither this exercise program nor any other exercise program should
be followed without first consulting a health care professional. If you have any special
conditions requiring attention, you should consult with your health care professional
regularly regarding possible modification of the program contained in this book.

Text copyright © 2005 by Evan Cooper
Illustrations copyright © 2005 by Stacy Peterson

Little, Brown and Company

Time Warner Book Group
1271 Avenue of the Americas, New York, NY 10020
Visit our Web site at www.lb-teens.com

First Edition: April 2005

Library of Congress Cataloging-in-Publication Data

Cooper, Evan.
    Um, like . . . om : A girl goddess's guide to yoga / by Evan Cooper.— 1st ed.
        p. cm.
    ISBN 0-316-98001-3
    1. Hatha yoga for teenagers—Juvenile literature. 2. Teenage girls—Health and hygiene—
Juvenile literature. 3. Teenage girls—Mental health—Juvenile literature. I. Title.
RA781.7.C665 2005
613.7'046'08352—dc22

                                                          2004007397

        10   9   8   7   6   5   4   3   2   1

                        BIND RITE

            Printed in the United States of America

To my family, whom I love

FIRST AND FOREMOST, thank you to all of the wonderful girls whom I have been honored to teach and who contributed their stories to this heartfelt endeavor. A very special thanks to my loving, incomparable family and friends whose support has been essential to this process.

TO ALL OF THE TEACHERS IN MY LIFE, especially Guru Singh, Ana Forrest, my guardian angel — Sat Kirin Kaur Khalsa, Seal, Saul David Raye, Mary Edwards, Hosea Johnson, and James Todd King. Thank you for your guidance and inspiration.

SPECIAL SHOUT-OUTS to Johnny-boy Sousa, Lauren and Ashley Steinberg (my mini-goddess editors), Renee Raphael, Jennifer Grandy, Romelia Martinez, Ettienne Eckhart, Lisa Hashim, Juby Becker, Laura Mendelow, Jordan Catapano, Andy Rafal, Monica Rizzo, and to the wonderful Eliza, Abby, and Beth Gold.

TO ALL OF THOSE WHO HELPED turn an idea into a reality and without whom this book would not have been published: Gary Stuart (a million thank you's for your faith in me), to my literary agent, Dan Strone, for coming to my rescue and being the Man; and to my hardworking editors Mary Gruetzke and Sangeeta Mehta — thank you for all of your guidance, input, and enthusiasm.

LAST, BUT ESPECIALLY NOT LEAST, to the greatest writer, mentor, and friend a girl could ever dream of having: Thank you, Todd Gold, for believing in me, making me laugh, and teaching me, by example, how to be a rock star!

What makes this world so great is that we are free to express ourselves.

—Frank Cooper (my poppy)

TABLE OF CONTENTS

Bend and be straight.

—Lao-tzu

Introduction

> When you are inspired by some great purpose . . .
> you find yourself in a new, great and wonderful world.
> —Patanjali (c. BC 200)

·········· WELCOME TO MY WORLD

Okay, I'm sitting here in my bedroom, trying to figure out what is going on in this crazy life of mine.

Last night I went out to dinner with a really hot guy, and he hasn't called me back. I'm so bummed. And get this: Instead of hearing from Mr. He's-So-Hot-That-He-Could-Be-the-Rest-of-My-Life, this dorky guy who I met at a party after dinner has left something like seventeen annoying messages on my machine, and I don't even know how he got my number. It's causing me major chocolate deprivation. But if I give in to the urge and devour my secret stash of M&Ms, I will hate myself.

I am on the verge of a freak-out.

What do I do?

I take a nice, long, breath of O_2. I mean a long breath.

No, not better. They want to feel their *best*, and so should you.

Yoga will help you through the situations in life that create anxiety, stress, and confusion, including relationships, your friends, studying for tests, parents, and PMS. It will help make a bad day good and a good day great. Put aside any preconceptions you have about yoga. It's not just for one kind of girl—it's for all of us. Don't let the way you think you look or feel prevent you from taking a chance on doing something that will help you. Look, my dad thinks I'm out of my mind for practicing yoga. But he doesn't think Colin Farrell is cute either.

This book speaks directly to you girls. The series of exercises I am about to teach you is devised to lead you into a deep sense of calm and confidence, that sense of knowing you'll be okay. This is what I call faith.

A master yogi once said, "When the student is ready, the teacher will appear." Through the simple act of picking up this book, you have shown that you're ready to learn, ready to change, ready to feel your best.

········How I Became a Yogini

> I once was lost but now am found, was blind but now I see.
> —"Amazing Grace" by John Newton (1725–1807)

Yeah, I know that song has nothing to do with learning to do yoga. Or does it? In my case, it does. It wasn't until I lost my eyesight that I was introduced to yoga. I literally had to go blind before I learned how to see. At the scariest time in my life, I became a student who was ready to learn how to "see" in my mind's eye when my real vision had failed me. That is when my first yoga teacher appeared. Let me explain.

By the time I was seventeen, I was getting sick very frequently. My life had been pretty normal up to then, if "normal" means you have a boy's name, your parents are divorced, and you wish just one cute boy would pay attention to you. Then, all of a sudden, I was tired all the time and felt depressed for no reason.

Although I was a "good kid" who did well in school and was active and artistic, I was doing some not-so-healthy things, like starving myself during the school day, not getting enough sleep at night, and letting my emotions get the best of me at every opportunity. You couldn't tell from looking at me, but I was so in control, I was *out* of control.

Then one night I woke up at three in the morning with a raging headache. I rolled out of bed and stumbled into the bathroom to swallow a few aspirin. I was upset with the person I saw in the mirror. I reprimanded myself for how unhealthy it was to have smoked cigarettes with my friends a few days earlier. "That's why your head hurts," I said.

By the following morning, my head and more specifically my left eye really began to hurt. My vision had also become increasingly blurry. I was totally freaked out.

I became even more frightened when, after a few doctors' appointments and several brain scans and blood tests, the doctors told me that my optic nerve was swollen and there was nothing they could do but wait and hope that my sight returned over time.

But teenagers aren't programmed to wait. Everything has to be *now!* And hope? You hope you get a decent grade on math tests. You hope your boobs are great. You hope you get a date to the prom. You don't *hope* to get your eyesight back.

Fortunately, my mother wasn't content to just wait. She took me to Dr. S. Khalsa, a specialist in alternative forms of medicine such as herbs, acupuncture, and homeopathy. Within several minutes of my first visit, the doctor asked if I had ever done yoga. I shook my head no. He then told me about yoga. He described it as special exercises in controlled breathing and movement that help people heal themselves.

He saw my eyes—yes, even my bad eye—brighten. I was intrigued.

"You can make a full recovery," Dr. Khalsa said confidently, "if you follow my instructions. Eat healthy. No drinking or smoking. Take all prescribed medicines and herbs. And practice yoga."

I would have done anything to get my sight back.

"Where do I practice?" I asked.

At that very moment, I became the student. I was ready to learn, and what I'd learn would change my life.

Dr. Khalsa introduced me to my teacher, Guru Singh. I signed up for a class. As I spread my blanket among the seasoned yoga students who were stretching, loosening up, and meditating, I was intimidated. An hour later, though, I was hooked. Guru Singh was an amazing teacher who had an aura, or glow, around him that was bright, intense, and spiritual. Just being around him made me feel as if I was a spiritual being. Over time I learned that I *was* a spiritual being. You are too. We all are.

Anyway, yoga quickly became part of my weekly routine, and my life started to change. I grew healthier and stronger with each stretch, breath, and positive thought. Gradually, my eyesight improved too.

Interestingly, I noticed I also became more centered, grounded, and energetic. Yoga was a positive outlet for the things that had always driven me crazy. I stopped obsessing about what I ate and how I looked. I didn't throw out my hair straightener, but if my hair was frizzy, so what? I'd work with it. I found myself wanting to hang out with friends and meet new people rather than zone out in front of MTV and sleeping my weekends away. If someone asked me what I was into, I now had an answer that made me sound smart, interesting, and cool. I also had something that actually made me feel good. And that's pretty important!

What It Means to Be a Teenager

CHAPTER 1

We know what we are, but know not what we may be.
— Shakespeare

•••••••• PRESSURES, CHALLENGES, AND BEING COOL

What does it mean to be a teenager?

It means you literally zip through one of the strangest, wackiest, most traumatic, exciting, and fun times of your life. It means one minute you think your life is fantastic, and the next minute you think it sucks; one minute you're having the time of your life, the next you're wishing someone would just put you out of your misery. But then, at least according to everyone over thirty, you spend the rest of your life wishing you could do it again, zits and all.

It's a weird time. You're not a kid, yet you're barely an adult. Your parents don't seem to understand anything about you. No one *gets* it. I mean, you go from buying underwear in the children's department to Victoria's Secret. Explain that to the sweet neighbor lady asking when you got so big. You freak out constantly over the injustices teenagers face daily. You're old enough to drive your little brother to soccer practice on a Tuesday afternoon, but you're not allowed to take the car out to the movies with friends on a Friday night. You can stay up past 11:00 studying for exams, but you're not old enough to stay out past 11:00 with the gorgeous captain of the football team.

Those are just the public battles. It would take a whole team of therapists, stylists, hairdressers, social planners, dermatologists, and personal trainers to work out your extremely private struggles with wearing the right clothes and keeping your skin clear, your hair done, your look fresh, your body perfect, your social calendar full...and, not to forget, staying on top of the effort to get into a good college eventually. God, I still remember the last time someone said, "Remember, grades count." I wanted to turn around and say, "Yeah, and so does this outfit."

Ironically, at the same time you're trying to fit in, you're also trying to break away from the pack and establish your independence. Sometimes I think there should be an official National Teenagers' Day when you simply get to call a time-out. You don't do your hair, you let your skin break out, and you wear a T-shirt that says, "Cool Girl Off Duty Today." In yoga terms, that would be like a great big exhale.

Girls, get ready to kick off your Uggs and breathe a sigh of relief because anyone can find happiness simply by getting in touch with her own unique self! Yoga helps you do that.

Becoming a Spiritual Warrior

If you aren't prepared to see your life go from just so-so to flipping fantastic, then I'd stay clear away from doing any yoga. Because doing yoga will change you. It will change you for the better. Maybe not necessarily in a Julia Roberts-in-*Pretty Woman*-ride-off-into-the-sunset-in-a-limo-with-Richard Gere sort of way, but in a deeper, more meaningful way. The most amazing changes you'll experience aren't on the outside, they're on the inside. Yoga has the power to transform a struggling teen into a spiritual warrior. Okay, hold up a sec and I'll explain.

A "spiritual warrior" is a girl (or guy) who trusts in her spirit so firmly that nothing can knock her down. You don't have to do anything like join a convent or the military to be a spiritual warrior. You don't even have to have any religion at all. All you have to do is learn to perceive your own beauty, really see your magnificence. A spiritual warrior is one who revels in the ordinary, lightens up during the heavier times, and lives a fun, full life. But let me give you some examples of real-life spiritual warriors — my students.

Sara is a regular student of mine who I first met at a class I taught in Studio City, California. She is a giggly, radiant, and energetic girl. You can immediately tell that she also has a much deeper, sensitive side when you look in her eyes. When she first came to class, she told me that one of her greatest stresses was the pressure to get good grades in school. So we worked on that. And we worked on feeling centered in general. Fast-forward a few months and Sara now handles these pressures with more ease and grace, and she reminds herself that grades are important but they do not define her worth as a human being. Just knowing this makes Sara a spiritual warrior. Choosing to come to yoga rather than hide under her covers when the going gets tough makes her a spiritual warrior. The process of growing up is messy. She knows this and chooses over and over to love the mess rather than lament it. She chooses her spirit over her suffering.

Check out Ashley's story. When Ashley first came to my class, she was so super skinny, she was *not-eating* herself to death. Yoga for Ashley became more than an exercise or a profound philosophy — it became a path to discovering her spirit. Before coming to yoga, Ashley was so obsessed with her body and all her perceived faults that she completely failed to see the wonderment of her own inner girl. And when she got a glimpse of how brilliant her inner self was, she was shocked, then inspired, then ready to become a healthy girl, a spiritual warrior! She fought the inner demons that were about to lead her to an eating disorder, and she won. Now Ashley sees her body as a shrine for her spirit rather than her worst enemy.

I will introduce you to many other girls who are true spiritual warriors. Some do yoga for fun, some for exercise, others to help conquer personal battles. They are all creative and independent girls who, through yoga, have found out how cool it can be to follow their own heartsong. They're girls just like you.

You're on your way to becoming a spiritual warrior!

CHAPTER 2

What Is Yoga?

Your work is to discover your world and then
with all your heart give yourself to it.
— Buddha

• • • • • • STANDING ON YOUR HEAD, PRETZEL LOGIC, AND BREATHING

So let's talk about yoga. Like, what exactly is it?
Yoga is an ancient science from India that
includes physical, mental, and spiritual action. It
is an exercise, a philosophy, and if you want it to
be, a way of life. It's definitely part of a healthy
life. Yoga is not a religion. You do not have to be
Buddhist, Hindu, or Sikh to practice. I know
Christians, Jews, and Muslims who are all avid yogis. Nor do you have to
look like Cameron Diaz, Drew Barrymore, or the Olsen twins to do yoga.
Whether you are fat or thin, tall or short, silly or serious, you can do yoga.
    "Yoga" is a word in the ancient Indian language of Sanskrit that means
"union," and it is through the practice of yoga that you unite your mind,

body, and spirit. Let me explain it like this: On a bad day, none of them are in unison. Your mind is crying out for chocolate, your body doesn't want it, and your spirit knows it will wilt quicker than an old flower if any of those candy bars reach your thighs. At your best, your mind, body, and spirit are as perfectly coordinated as tennis star Anna Kournikova's tan, outfit, and backhand. And who wouldn't want to feel that in sync? And you don't even have to worry about having the perfect moves, because the yoga I will teach you was designed specifically for you.

Because yoga is over 4,000 years old and from the other side of the world, it was a challenge for us modern Westerners to fully understand what it was really all about. Originally written in Sanskrit the philosophy of yoga was something very foreign and ancient compared to our current-day, high-tech world. So we made some alterations. Basically, Americans took the traditional form of yoga, flipped it around, bent it, and shaped it into a practice made more for us. We did yoga to our yoga!

·········YOGA, THE WESTERN WAY

It's cool when you can take something completely unfamiliar to you and make it your own. And with yoga, we have taken a very important concept and adapted it into something we can apply to our own lives. When Westerners modified traditional systems of yoga to a style that was more user-friendly, it opened up a whole new world for those of us looking for a way to chill out. For the most part, we kept the basic philosophy and physical poses and left the more abstract, intellectual stuff back in India. A centered mind and peaceful spirit are still the intention, but now, instead of something only wise old men on mountaintops in India can do, yoga is something anyone and everyone can benefit from.

The downside to having made yoga our own is that when word has to travel far, it usually loses some of its original meaning. (Remember the game "telephone" where you whispered something in the ear of the person sitting next to you, and then by the time it reached the last person, what was first said comes out a funnier, inaccurate version of the original? It was like something got lost in the translation.) Well, by the time yoga got over here, it had become a whole new version of the original. As we added things like rock music and focused more on achieving buns of steel, we focused less and less on the spiritual aspect of yoga. Typical of our Western world, we instinctively focused on the visible outer effects of yoga and a lot less on yoga's subtle inner effects.

Another downside to our adaptation of yoga is that newcomers often think that it's some sort of fruit-loopy, made-up mumbo jumbo where we all float around with our heads in the clouds. Yoga is about tapping into our spirit and believing in the things we cannot see, but it is also about real, factual, and physical teachings.

··········SCIENCE + SPIRITUALITY = YOGA

> Growing up in a house full of doctors, I was trained to make
> the so-called "right" decision by weighing all of my options.
> But things can't always be resolved by scientific reasoning.
> Like when I have an important decision to make, I try to make
> the most logical choice. But in the end, my heart always
> seems to speak louder than my head.
> —Renee Raphael, Hollywood stylist to the stars

Who knew a fashionista could be as insightful as she is in vogue? Whether she realizes it or not, Renee's dilemma speaks directly about the balance of logic and emotion, science and spirit. This is what yoga is about: science and reason, spirituality and intuition. It's about the balance of everything in our world, but ultimately about listening to the sound of your own heart. Proven reality is important, but what is true *for you* is what is most important. And no two people will share the exact same truth. Thankfully, there are just as many variations of yoga as you probably have shoes.

There are many different styles of yoga, with just as many origins. For example, there is Raja yoga (royal yoga), Mantra yoga (the yoga of sound), Bhakti yoga (devotional yoga), and Hatha yoga (physical). Much of what I will teach you is Hatha (pronounced Hut-hah) yoga. There are subtle differences among the various branches of yoga, but all forms of yoga are rooted in one fundamental principle—the breath. Air and the energy contained within it, or what in yoga terms is referred to as prana, is our life force. Without it, we can't exist. I know it sounds too simple to be true, but if you learn to breathe properly, you can learn to control your thoughts and emotions.

The physical positions, or asanas, are fundamental to the practice of Hatha yoga. These exercises stretch and tone your muscles, increase flexibility, stimulate your glands and organs, and generally relax your body. Not only are they fun, but they will also help you move through your life experiences with a greater sense of ease and confidence with your body. The word "asana" also means "to be present." Which makes sense because you really have to be present when doing yoga. Space out and you'll lose your balance. And falling on your face is never a pretty sight.

We will also meditate together. Actually, I will teach you how to meditate, since it is a deeply personal, solo activity you do in order to get in touch with the inner quiet of your spirit. Your spirit is what we want to nourish, protect, and celebrate. Often, just chanting the word "OM" is enough to begin to move out of your hectic life and into the realm of relaxation. By the way, "OM" is the sound the universe makes when it's in perfect harmony, and it's the very same sound you hear on your inner radio when you tune in to the right frequency.

But I have to stop myself here. I hate it when I start sounding like a spaced-out, New Age know-it-all. Take away my strappy platform sandals when I get like that. Let me simply say this: Once you are in tune with your spiritual self, there isn't anything that you can't get through. You may fall apart at times, but you will know that ultimately you are a part of the world's unifying energy and everything will be okay.

So what do you need to start? You need a sticky mat or blanket or, if you are at home, a soft spot on the floor. Carpet will do nicely. Put on some loose, flexible, comfortable clothes. You want to feel free to bend and stretch.

You will also need a nice dose of patience, since it is crucial that you **practice yoga at your own pace.** Remember, yoga is not a competitive sport. Start slow. Have faith in your ability to learn, grow, and advance. No amount of peace of mind is worth a pulled muscle.

And most importantly, you need an open mind. I'm not kidding. It doesn't matter if you've taken ballet since you were four or if you've never touched your toes in your life. It doesn't matter if you are the head cheerleader, you're a Goth chick, or you're taking a break from Jenny Craig—anyone can use yoga as a tool to enhance her life. You simply have to start the journey.

Yoga is waiting for *you.*

Grab your mats, and let's get this party started!

CHAPTER 3

Learning to Breathe

A student approached the head monk of a Zen monastery to ask how he could alleviate himself of his suffering. The monk simply responded, "If you can breathe in...you can breathe out."

—Ancient oral anecdote

Breathing is the single most important aspect of practicing yoga. Why? Because it is essential to life, and the practice of yoga mirrors how you live your life. In fact, in Sanskrit, the word for life and breath is the exact same: prana. In order to live, we need to breathe; in order to meditate or practice yoga, we need to breathe correctly.

So let's learn to breathe.

I know it may sound crazy that we need to learn to do something as automatic as breathing, but the truth is, more often than not, we do not breathe correctly—or at least in a way that fills us with the greatest amount of oxygen possible.

So let's go through the easy-to-follow steps.

········HOW TO BREATHE

1. Find a place to sit comfortably with your legs crossed in front of you in Easy Pose. Alternatively, you can sit in Lotus Pose, the classic seated asana in which each foot rests on the opposite thigh.

2. Straighten your spine, let your shoulders gently relax down away from your ears, and slightly lower your chin toward your chest.

3. Place one hand on your belly button and the other on your lower back so you can feel the navel point expand as you inhale.

4. With your mouth closed and your lower jaw relaxed, inhale and exhale slowly through your nose. (Think of your tummy as a balloon. You want to fill and deflate it with every breath.)

5. Envision that you are breathing into the lower part of your lungs, filling them up from bottom to top. Take a long, deep, expanding inhale and a slow, complete exhale.

Okay, so I know that it's hard to focus on breathing when it's something that happens whether you think about it or not. But just try it for a week and tell me that you don't have more energy, last longer at track practice or cheerleading, concentrate longer doing your algebra homework, and stay calmer in front of the hot guy from third period. Don't worry about becoming frustrated if you can't get it right at first.

Most of us have a fairly small lung capacity from lack of use, but as you deepen your breath and expand your lungs with every breath, over time, your capacity to breathe will grow tremendously.

Ujjayi: The Special Yogic Breath

Ujjayi (pronounced u-JAI-ee) breathing is the one method of breathing specifically practiced while doing yoga. It is a controlled form of inhaling and exhaling done through the nose, while allowing the breath to create a soft sound in back of the throat. Imagine how it feels when you fog up a mirror by breathing on it through your mouth. Well, that's exactly the sensation of Ujjayi breathing, only done through the nose. (It should sound the way that creepy *Star Wars* character Darth Vader breathes.) You'll quickly find that when you practice Ujjayi, you'll end up paying less attention to how your butt looks in your lowrider jeans and more on the rhythm of your breath and the sensation of air in your body. The Ujjayi breath is about breathing in the life force, or prana, in the air so that we can practice and live more fully.

> **FYI (Fun Yoga Information):**
> When you breathe deeply enough to draw the air into the lower third of your lungs, you get seven times the oxygen you normally would have taken in!!

........• BREATHWORK, OR *PRANAYAMA*

Energizing Breath: Breath of Fire (Kapala-bhati)

When you're tired — mind and body need a quick pick-me-up — or you just need to clear your head, Breath of Fire is one of the coolest practices because it is said by ancient Indian philosophy to cure many illnesses. If you've never felt like you were floating before, you will now!

1. Sit in Easy Pose, legs crossed. Place your hands on your lower belly so you can feel the "pumping" sensation of the breath.
2. Take three to five long, deep breaths, in and out, through the nose. (You should feel your belly filling up and then emptying out, as if you had your hands on a balloon.)
3. After your last long inhale, do ten fast exhales, allowing short inhales between each exhale. (Repeat two or three times.)

Note: If you begin to feel light-headed while you practice Breath of Fire, gently bring your head down to your knees and take a few long, deep breaths. This one takes some practice, so be patient with yourself!

Cooling Breath: Sitali Pranayam

This is a "cooling breath" and it will slow your heart rate, allowing you to calm yourself and regain your focus.

1. Inhale through your mouth with a curled tongue, letting your tongue stick out a little. (So it's like you're sucking the air in through a straw—that is your tongue!)
2. Gently exhale through your nose. Repeat ten to fifteen times.

Balancing Breath:
Alternate Nostril Breathing (Nadi-shodhana)

This is a technique used by yogis for hundreds of years to help balance their minds and create a more centered feeling in the body.

1. Sit in a comfortable position, spine tall and straight.
2. With your right hand, place your thumb on your right nostril and your ring (or fourth) finger on your left nostril. (Tuck your first and middle fingers down.)

3. Now, closing the right nostril with your thumb, inhale through your left nostril for five counts.

4. Close your left nostril, and exhale through your right nostril for five counts.

5. Now inhale through the right nostril for five counts.

6. Exhale through the left nostril for five counts....

And continue in the same pattern for anywhere from one minute to fifteen minutes!

> **FYI**
>
> Did you know that each nostril is directly linked to the side of the brain it's on!

MEDITATION: TURNING *IT* ON

Maybe you have meditated before, but I'm going to assume this is your first journey into your inner universe. You can meditate right away, but it takes practice to do it well. Initially, though, think of meditation as listening to a radio. You are tuning in to the song of the universe, the best song ever.

How do you start? How do you do it? I'll explain.

- ❁ Find a comfortable place to sit. Pick a large, flat, square cushion and label it your "meditation cushion." Or use a favorite blanket, folding it up once or twice.
- ❁ Sit in Easy Pose or Lotus Pose. (Sit in Lotus Pose by placing each foot on top of the opposite thigh, rather than under the thighs.)
- ❁ Close your eyes, sit up straight, and let your shoulders and chin relax down, as you did when learning to breathe properly.
- ❁ Now relax and breathe naturally.
- ❁ With your eyes closed, focus your attention on the center of your forehead. This spot is commonly known as your "third eye," or sixth chakra (see p. 30), the birthplace of your intuition.
- ❁ Bring your palms together at the center of your chest in the prayer position. Now inhale deeply and recite — either aloud or to yourself — a tuning-in mantra.

•••••• WHAT? YOU DON'T HAVE A MANTRA?

You don't even know what a mantra is? Don't freak out. This isn't a test.

A mantra is something your mind projects. It's a picture, a thought, an affirmation, a color, a word, a feeling. Mantras come in all shapes, sizes, and languages. You have your choice of those written in Sanskrit to traditional Buddhist chants. If you don't read Sanskrit or know any traditional Buddhist chants, don't worry. Your mantra can be a phrase as simple as "I'm awesome," "I am brilliant," "I am pretty," or even "The only opinion that matters is my own!"

The first mantra I learned, given to me by a Sikh yogi, goes, "Ong Namo Guru Dev Namo." It means, "I honor the teacher within my own being." Pronounce it just as it looks: NAH-mo.

Another favorite that holds the same meaning, except that it is from the Hindu culture, is "Om Namah Shivaya." I'll give you a few more in later meditations. But don't sweat the pronunciation.

Whatever mantra you choose, repeat it three times. Then take a few minutes to breathe, relax for about a minute or two, and feel the shift in you that has taken place. Breathe in, exhale, breathe in, and exhale. Good.

Now you are ready to practice, perform, or just deal with, you know, whatever's on your mind.

WHAT THE HECK ARE "CHAKRAS"?

We all have seven energy centers, or "chakras," which literally means "wheels." Each chakra corresponds to a different spot on the body, starting from the base of the spine and moving up to the top of the head. If you have trouble conceptualizing what an "energy center" actually is, think about it as an invisible force that enables your body to function. When the forces or chakras are balanced, you function at your best. When you experience an imbalance in one or more of your chakras, which we all do at one point or another, you may feel sluggish, sick, or simply "off." Here is a description of the chakras and how they each relate to your life:

1st chakra (red): Root chakra. Located at the base of your spine, this chakra relates to our basic need to survive.

2nd chakra (orange): Sexuality, creativity, procreation, need for approval, self-acceptance.

3rd chakra (yellow): Navel point and solar plexus. Power, control, growth.

4th chakra (green): Heart center. Relates to our experience and expression of love and compassion.

5th chakra (blue): Located at the throat. Understanding, communication, truth.

6th chakra (indigo): Third Eye point. Intuition, projection, wisdom.

7th chakra (violet): Crown of the head. Allowance (I'm not talking money here!

It is your ability to go with the flow of the universe), self-realization. Relates to our personal connection to the entire universe.

Sometimes an **8th chakra (white)** is recognized as the "aura" or energy field that extends around us and reflects our mental and physical state of being.

So how does breathing properly affect these energy centers? By moving prana throughout the body, you create an open space within yourself, and this allows energy to move freely throughout your body. Imagine yourself as a really tall tree. How do you keep the tiny leaves on the tops of your branches green and alive and beautiful? You suck the nutrients up from your roots (ah, the first chakra!), up through the trunk of your body (your spine!), until they reach the very tips of the tops of all your leaves (your crown chakra!). Same idea with your body's energy centers. If you awaken your chakras through yoga, you can literally draw in the earth's energy when you breathe.

FYI: KUNDA-WHO?

"Kundalini" (pronounced koon-da-LEE-nee) is the name of the energy that lies dormant, or asleep, at the base of your spine. Yoga awakens this energy so that it can be free to rise up through all of your chakras. It is symbolized by a serpent.

YOGA PREP:

A few key things to remember throughout your yoga practice:

- Flex your feet (this keeps the leg muscles working).
- Relax your neck.
- Roll your shoulders down away from your ears.
- Keep your butt tucked under.
- Breathe, breathe, breathe!

Yoga and Fear

Yoga and Fear

CHAPTER 4

Yoga and Fear

> Twenty years from now you will be more disappointed by the things that you didn't do than by the ones you did do. So throw off the bowlines. Sail away from the safe harbor. Catch the trade winds in your sails. Explore. Dream. Discover.
>
> — Mark Twain

FEAR VS. FAITH: THE ULTIMATE CHOICE

Fear is that sensation that makes you grab tightly onto your seat. It's the feeling that makes your stomach turn and your hands shake and your heart race. It's the feeling of having no idea what's next but knowing that whatever it is could be more painful than flopping your audition for the school play. It is also an attachment to the material world, to your physical being, to a reality that is illusory and temporary. This is because nothing in the material world, not even our bodies, is around forever. Sure, we're given a physical body, a form within which to chill for, hopefully, a good sixty to eighty years. It's a form that will drink a few sodas, and wear a few tube tops. But it is our spirits that ensure us our immortality. Hot as it is, even Ashton Kutcher's body is gonna wrinkle up one day. But if you believe in energy, then you will understand why our spirits never die. And that's where we need to place our faith: in the eternal, unchanging aspects of life, in our spirits.

It's kind of like when your face has totally broken out or you realize that you forgot to shave your legs and you're sporting a miniskirt. You might be on the embarrassed side, but it's not like you are afraid you will lose your friends over it. You have faith beyond that superficial stuff; you know that you are still the same beautiful person on the inside, and it is certainly not the end of the world. Once you choose to place your energy in your faith and not in your fear, something magical happens: the fear goes away. Yoga helps us to do this.

My friends often compliment me on my strong sense of faith and ability to take risks, so they find it hard to believe that I can be afraid to get on a plane. But it's true, I am afraid to fly. Thankfully, yoga helps me deal...and fly! One night, my friend Jen sat me down and confronted me about my fear. "You, of all people, should know that what is meant to be will be, so why stress yourself out over it?" I don't know why I continue to hold on to such a deep and pervasive fear, but to this day, I practice to overcome it. If I didn't do this and I allowed the fear to control me, I'd give up vacations to avoid flying, and I'd lose out on the adventures of life.

One of my students, Renee, had planned to spend a semester of her junior year with her best friend at a New York City high school. But when her friend came down with mono and had to cancel her plans to go to New York at the last minute, Renee had to decide whether she would go alone. "Even though I was scared, I really wanted to face this challenge," Renee proudly recalled in class one day. I was impressed. Immediately, I thought about how I was afraid just to go on an upcoming yoga retreat in Hawaii because of the five-hour flight involved. And it occurred to me right then and there that if I were to give in to my fear of flying (and give up a rockin' trip to Maui), I would have to stop writing this book. I would have to stop teaching lessons that I wasn't prepared to practice myself.

The thing is, fear not only affects the practical aspects of life but our entire physical and mental well-being. It's not just about facing our fear, but dealing with it on a deeper "soul" level—which is where the balancing effects of yoga come into play. Often, we experience our fears as an imbalance in our bodies: we get sick or we sleep or we become overly anxious. For example, my fear of flying usually manifests itself in the form of a sore throat. Sound crazy? Think of it this way: our bodies and minds are interconnected, so even a simple thought, emotion, or fear can affect how the body feels.

Fear is related to the fifth chakra, our center of understanding (see the chakra chart on p. 31). This is also our center of faith in divine will over personal will. So when I begin to fear an upcoming flight, I lose touch with the greater force at work and the larger plan of my life. My fifth chakra falls out of balance, and I get a sore throat!

There is a special mantra for protection that I find especially soothing when I feel afraid. You just repeat the following mantra three times either aloud or to yourself.

Ad Guray Nameh   (Ahhd Gu-ray Na-may)
Jugad Guray Nameh   (Ju-god Gu-ray Na-may)
Sat Guray Nameh   (Sat Gu-ray Na-may)
Siri Guru Devay Nameh   (Si-ri Gu-ru De-vay Na-may)

This mantra, written in a language similar to Sanskrit called Gurmukhi, means "I bow to the wisdom of the universe and to the wisdom within my own being." It will protect you in any situation. Sikh yogis use it for protection while traveling. Believe me, whenever I fly, I repeat this mantra before those plane wheels even leave the runway. I also use this one when I'm a passenger in my younger brother's car, 'cause he drives about as well as I cook.

FYI: SAY WHAT? THE POWER OF PRAYER

Who would have thought that just saying something out loud could make it true? That is exactly the power of a prayer or mantra. *Mantra* means your "mind's projection." And when you project an idea out into the universe, it will always be reflected back in one form or another. Chanting a mantra is like getting all dolled up and then looking in the mirror; if you put your best out there, then that's what you'll see staring back at you!

••••• NATURAL DISASTERS VS. WARDROBE TRAGEDIES (BIG FEARS VS. LITTLE FEARS)

Fear is a necessary part of being alive. It warns us of danger and sometimes helps us to make better choices. Of course, fear of wearing the wrong outfit to the dance and fear of world war are two entirely different talk shows. This is when you need to take a long, deep breath and determine whether your fear is rational. I think we should keep a sprinkle of fear in our pockets, just so we have it for the times it's really necessary, and then throw the rest of our useless fears out! Practice being fearless on your lesser anxieties. Go on the triple-loop roller coaster, babysit for the kids who live at the scary, creaky mansion down the block, go bungee jumping! Then, when it comes time to face your fears of bigger, scarier situations, you'll be ready! And yoga can help you prepare yourself for a life of fearlessness—or *abhaya*, for all you Sanskrit lovers.

> Do not anticipate trouble, or worry about what may never happen. Keep in the sunlight.
> —Benjamin Franklin

These exercises stimulate the kidneys, the adrenal glands, and the internal organs of the lower three chakras, where we store fear and anxiety. These will help to ease and release those fears.

Butterfly Pose (Baddha Konasana)

1. Sit up tall and straight.
2. Bring the soles of your feet together so your knees fall to the side. Press the balls of your feet together and flex your toes back.

Forward Bend in Butterfly Pose

1. While sitting in Butterfly Pose, inhale and lift your chest.
2. Now exhale, completely relaxing your head and neck down.
3. Slowly walk your hands out in front of your feet, bending forward.
4. Take five long, deep breaths.

Lying Down in Butterfly Pose
(Supta Baddha Konasana)

1. Lie flat on your back.
2. Bring the soles of your feet together
   and let your knees fall to the sides. (If
   it's more comfortable, you can put a pillow
   beneath each knee so your legs are supported.)
3. Breathe long and deep.

Bridge Pose (Setu Bandha Sarvangasana)

1. Lie on your back with your knees bent and your feet flat on the
   floor. (Make sure your feet are hip-width apart and not right next
   to each other.)
2. Place your hands at your sides, palms facedown on the ground.
3. Inhale deeply. Lift your butt and hips off the ground. (Squeeze
   those butt and leg muscles—work it, girl!)
4. Hold here for five long, deep
   breaths.

5. Slowly come down, lowering yourself from the top of your spine to the base of your spine.
6. Repeat three times.

•••••••••MEDITATION: FAITH OVER FEAR!

A good way to practice abhaya or fearlessness is to use your fifth chakra, the energy center located at your throat. How do you use your fifth chakra? You use your voice. Speaking from your heart is very powerful because you are taking formless thoughts and giving them a place in the physical world. We can actually tell the universe how we want our lives to work out and it will listen.

- ❁ Choose a song—any song—and sing, chant, or speak the words. Just use your voice, loud and strong. (Oh, and remember to close your bedroom door if you're at home!)
- ❁ Sing so loud that you drown out your fears. Sing so loud that there is no choice but to believe in what you have to say!

> FYI:
> I know you sing in the shower, girlfriend! You already incorporate aspects of yoga into your life and didn't even know it, did you?!

CHAPTER 5

Feeling Good

There is no way to happiness — happiness is the way.

—Buddha

• • • • • • NATURAL HIGH: WHAT IT FEELS LIKE

Allow me to introduce you to my drug of choice: yoga. It rocks. Why else do you think I do it every single day of my life? I've smoked a few times and tried all sorts of wicked drugs, and at the end of the day, all they do is leave you feeling worse than you started.

A few months ago, a girl named Rachel showed up to my class for the first time. One look in her eyes and I knew she was stoned out of her mind. After class, I asked Rachel if the next time she came to my class, she'd come sober. She was like, "How in the world did you know I was high?" And I was like, "Dude, been there, done that, had the munchies, suffered the consequences." I didn't chastise or give her one of those condescending "Don't do drugs, drugs are bad" lectures— I just did for her what I'm going to do for you now: I showed her, by example, how choosing to do yoga over drugs would give her the high of her life.

But I'll let Rachel tell you about her experience herself:

When I first heard about yoga for teens, I so didn't want to go. But I'd flaked on my friend Katie so many times that when she asked me to go a few times I just said "Fine" and went. She made it sound like she wanted me to go because it was fun, but really it was her way of trying to get me to stop smoking pot. I guess she hadn't smoked since she started doing yoga, so she thought I might not either. I was the biggest skeptic ever. I'm like the most unathletic person in the world. I can't even touch my toes. But I felt so good when we were through with the class that now I go all the time. Crazy, I know.

Because Rachel was so used to achieving a false sense of relaxation, when she got a taste of what a natural high, a yogic high, felt like, it was a huge awakening for her. "I don't even smoke now at parties or dances. Instead, I do some yoga at home before I go so I can feel as good as I did — no, *better* than when I did drugs. Actually, I feel the best I ever have!"

As she said "I never knew you could feel so incredible all on your own!" I was like, "Duh! I didn't make it up!"

I knew that, in just a few classes, Rachel would be hooked because instead of numbing her pain with drugs, she'd be facing it with yoga. I've always thought that the people who do the most to hide their pain are the ones who benefit the most from actually dealing with it. And believe it or not, when you practice yoga, you are taking all the pain in your world and squeezing it out of you, as if you were a sponge wringing yourself out. You are dealing with it.

•••••••DON'T HOLD IT IN

Dealing with your issues isn't always easy, especially when they have been hidden away deep inside your body for a long time. Sometimes we hold on to things we don't even realize we're holding on to. Many times, when you start practicing yoga, your body's flood gates will open up and emotion will come rushing out. You'll burst out laughing or even discover a gush of tears streaming their way down your face. That's your body letting go. It's a good thing. It's tension we've built up in our bodies and now can release. It's a big part of why yoga makes you feel freer, lighter, higher.

Don't be afraid to let your stuff out either. If you want to howl in the middle of yoga class, then do it. (Just make sure it's not during a meditation or deep relaxation!) Most people think that only the weak show their emotions, when really, it takes a strong person to show her vulnerability to the world. And when you cram your grief down deep enough, it turns into disease. Maybe nothing big, but why get sick just to maintain a tough facade. Trust me, nothing feels as good as letting it all out into the open. There is no hurt so painful, no problem so big that you can't overcome it if you use yoga to help you through. Even you gals who don't have a care in the world, or those of you who are already quite athletic or naturally laid-back, can find some peace of mind by doing a little yoga when the going gets rough.

None of my girls knows this better than Jenny. Healthy and strong, she's a real powerhouse yogi—always going for it. She's seventeen now, but when she was fifteen, Jenny went from being an all-state runner at her high school to one sick little girl. She knew something was wrong with her body. From her head to her toes, she could hear her body screaming out for help, but nothing could keep this ultra-competitive, very determined racer from the track. You know when you want something really badly—so badly that you will do anything to get it? Well, that's how Jenny felt about racing in an upcoming marathon. So she kept training, popped a couple of aspirin every time the pain became too much to bear, and slowly became more and more depressed by her diminishing health.

At the same time, Jenny had been recruited by several colleges— all offering her a spot to run on their respective track teams. She was excited, but more than excited, she was terrified. Moving away from home and her best friends would be hard enough. But the added challenge of everyone counting on her to set records on the track? On the inside, Jenny says she felt like, "Oh my god, how in the world am I going to handle all the pressure?" But rather than talk about her feelings, she tucked them away. All her fears of moving on, of success, of going to a college where she'd have even more pressure to win races, were suppressed deep inside herself. And that's when Jenny went from feeling bad to worse. What began as a lack of energy and random stomachaches that left her doubled over in pain came to a head when Jenny's body finally just completely gave out on her. She barely had the energy to walk, much less run.

Turns out, a few doctors' appointments later, she found out that she had a disease called celiac disease. Her stomach couldn't digest certain foods properly, so instead of gaining energy from eating, she was literally running on empty. It was almost as if she had stuffed so much emotion into her body, it didn't have room for anything else. Jenny's body had been telling her something was wrong for a long time, and now it was way past time to do something about it.

With a proper diagnosis, a change in her diet, and the courage to start speaking up about feelings of being overwhelmed, Jenny slowly started to heal. And that's when she came to my yoga class. It was a big turning point for her because unlike being a runner, being a yogini required self-compassion and listening to her body, instead of ignoring herself, pushing through the pain, or stuffing it away. Slowly, Jenny got her disease under control, and after learning how to honor her body, she has begun to run again. It took beating herself down in order for Jenny to learn to build herself back up. But you don't have to get horribly ill in order for you to find balance in your life. You don't have to suffer to justify wanting to feel good.

There are tons of ways to medicate or numb ourselves so we don't feel our pain. We ignore our bodies, we do drugs, we go to all extremes. Even though it takes a little effort to unroll your sticky mat and get the blood pumping, yoga will give you a buzz more powerful than any drug, any drink, or any hot date ever could. Then again, yoga isn't all about getting a quick buzz—it's about feeling the very best you can, physically, mentally, and emotionally, for as long as you can.

•••••••• YOGA FOR PHYSICAL WELL-BEING

Horse Stance ⭐

This asana will help you to strengthen your self-esteem, achieve your goals in life, and release any stress, sadness, or tension you are holding inside your body. It will also strengthen your knees, thighs, and core body.

1. Stand with your feet about three feet apart. Turn them out slightly, like a dancer would.
2. Bend your knees until your thighs are parallel to the ground. (This is when you'll start to feel the pose working in your legs!)
3. Check to make sure your knees are directly above your ankles.
4. Place your hands on your thighs and lean forward slightly.

Horse Stance with Lion's Breath

1. Inhale deeply, then stick your tongue out, open your mouth wide, and sigh or scream out any tension you have inside.
2. Repeat this several times, remembering that all the negative energy you release out with Lion's Breath, you must replace with positive energy through long, deep breaths afterward.

Cow/Cat Pose

Use this pose to warm up or wind down. It is especially good to do to feel a sense of peace and fluidity in our bodies. It is a pose that brings your body back into a neutral, calm state.

1. Sit on your hands and knees, like a four-legged animal (hands and knees hip-width apart).
2. Inhale and arch your back, letting your belly extend and fill up with air. Gently tilt your head and neck back.
3. Now exhale, and curve your back so it is high and rounded. Let your head and neck drop down. Suck your belly up toward the back of your spine.
4. Continue this in a flowing motion at a rhythmic pace — imagine your spine is as fluid as water. (Do anywhere from four to twenty times.)

Cow

Cat

Downward-Facing Dog (Adho Mukha Savasana)

One of the most widely practiced yoga poses, this is the ultimate asana because it give you the best high while it stretches and strengthens your entire body. Whenever you feel down or low-energy, do a quick dog and you'll feel worlds better.

1. Sit on your hands and knees (like you did in Cow/Cat).
2. Check your hands to make sure they are directly beneath your shoulders. Your knees should be directly beneath your hips.
3. Relax your head and neck down. Curl your toes under.
4. Inhale, then exhale and straighten your arms and legs (keeping them slightly bent until you become more comfortable with the pose).
5. Pull your belly in and lift your hips toward the ceiling.

Advanced Version:

6. Once you have slowly straightened your arms and legs, lower your heels so they are flat on the floor.
7. Always make sure you completely relax your neck. Just let it hang down. Your head won't fall off and roll away (I promise).

8. Stay for a few breaths, then lower yourself down onto all fours and sit back onto your heels in Child's Pose (see p. 61).

MEDITATION: "HEAL A SPOT"

Choose a spot on yourself that bothers you—either because it's a place where you feel pain, or you dislike the way it looks, or it's a spot that is numb and you can't feel it at all. These are all physical manifestations of something that's going on deep inside of us. We can figure out and heal those deeper wounds by **breathing life into those areas**—the surest path to healing our wounds and feeling good.

 Sit or lie in a comfortable position.
 Close your eyes.
 Choose your spot.
 Breathe long and deep, and focus on sending the breath directly into your spot. Envision the healing taking place as you breathe.
 Now send loving kindness to the spot. Inhale self-compassion, exhale self-hatred (in other words, only speak with great love and gentleness to yourself and your trouble spot).

Feeling Good About Yourself

CHAPTER 6

This above all; to thine own self be true.

— Shakespeare

• • • • • • • YOU AREN'T NUTS, YOU'RE A TEENAGE GIRL!

So the other day, I go to my closet to pick out something to wear to a friend's birthday party, and I'm a wreck. I can't find anything to wear. I have seven gazillion pairs of jeans and three hundred tops, and I can't find anything I like. What's wrong with me? Then I realize, that's exactly it! I'm not unhappy with my wardrobe, I'm unhappy with my own neurotic self! Can you relate to this, or what?

I don't need to tell you what it feels like to be a teenage girl. If you're reading this, then most likely you are one. You know how it feels. At least you know how *you* feel. I'm just here to confirm a few things, dispel a few myths, and let you know that you are not the only one who feels as if you'd be a whole lot happier if you packed up and hitched a flight to Tahiti. Running away from your world might seem like the answer, but you can't run away from yourself. You're still going to be a teenager when you arrive, even if you are lying on a beautiful beach.

When you're a teen, your highs are super high, and your lows are, well, if you got any lower, you'd hit Antarctica. And chances are, no one really talks about it. It probably seems more like every girl you know acts as if her life is Lindsey Lohan-perfect. This is simply an impossibility. Everyone, at one point or another during her teens, gets a little tweaked out emotionally. Things just feel off. Trust me, you're not alone.

Emotions are like the weather. Sooner or later, you're going to get rained on. Stick around, and the sun will dry you off. No matter how pretty you are, how rich you are, how popular you may be, everyone is subject to the laws of the universe. Same with emotions: everyone's got 'em. But if you can learn to feel good about who you are—with all your mood swings and breakouts and imperfections—then no storm will ever be strong enough to knock you off your feet. This is where yoga comes in. It can help you discover your inner strength. See, yoga is an equalizer. It mellows out the hormones that are raging and amps up the feel-good chemicals in the body that are slacking. Amazingly, you don't have to do anything except *do the yoga*. You don't even have to believe it will change you. It just will.

But don't take it from me alone—take it from Sunny, one of my most dedicated yoginis:

When I first decided I was going to enroll in a teen yoga

class, I never really thought how much it would affect my life and me. I thought I would be doing something healthy for my body and that it would be something fun to do with my best friend after school. But after the first class, I realized how much I really wanted yoga to be a part of my life. Yoga seemed to allow me to blossom into a more self-confident person. I am able to feel happier with who I am, not only physically but also on a deeper level. I am able to really accept who I am because during yoga I am able to tune in to what I am thinking deep down. I have become a more patient person and just a better person to talk to. One thing that my friends have noticed has changed about me since I began yoga is I became a less stressed-out person.

I love to listen to Sunny talk about how yoga has affected her life because she has grown so much in her yoga practice. Her experience really shows how powerful yoga can be in a girl's life. And the best part is that it's yours for the taking—all the yoga you want. (If only Macy's were so generous, right?) Girls like Sunny are proof that you have the ability to make your life what you want it to be and that yoga helps you to do this. Easier said than done, though, I know.

For some of you, it may take more than one yoga class, one moment of inspiration, one positive affirmation to really "get" yoga. No prob. It's kind of like when you hear a new song for the first time—you get a sense of it but may need to listen to it ten times before you think, *Oh my god, this is the best song ever!* If you do not take to yoga immediately, please, please, please do not go into self-bashing mode! This is a normal reaction to learning anything new. If you were teaching your friend how to work her new MP3 player and she didn't get it right away, would you call her a horrible and defective person? Give yourself a break. And give yourself the opportunity to feel good about yourself.

Now more than ever, you have to commit to being your own best friend, your number one fan, your own life's teacher. You know how you stare at the pages of famous chicks in *Teen People* mag and idolize them? Well, start staring in the mirror and idolize the girl you see in the reflection. My girls can tell you firsthand that nothing will get you through the rough times like having a really awesome sense of self.

> *Always* do the thing you are afraid to do.
> —Ralph Waldo Emerson

•••••••• THE COURAGE FACTOR

Ever realize how when you're feeling good about yourself, it's easier to take chances? Like at a school dance, when you're rocking in a miniskirt and platform shoes, and you know you look hot, and your girls are all around you — that's when you get the guts to go up and ask your crush to dance, right? When you feel good about yourself, you are more likely to risk losing an ounce of pride (or maybe even a little more) because you know there's a ton more where it came from. I heard this saying once: "If you are bored, risk something." And it makes a lot of sense because when you put yourself on the line, not only is there the potential for you to come out better but you are truly living life to its fullest.

My student Renee can attest to this. A self-described perfectionist, Renee was always preoccupied with how other people saw her and therefore never entirely happy just to be herself. Yoga changed that.

Doing yoga challenged me to go beyond my fears. I had a kind of performance anxiety about it. I didn't just want to go to a yoga class, I wanted to show everyone that I was the best at it. It took a couple of classes, but once I really got into the yoga, I just felt so good that I really didn't care what I looked like or who saw me.

You can't expect to just feel good about yourself without putting a little effort into it. Wouldn't it be nice if we were born with self-esteem the way we are born with two eyes, a nose, and lips? Unfortunately, we have to plant the seeds of self-confidence ourselves, then water them and tend them and allow ourselves to bloom into poised, confident people.

·········The Three Tenets

This seems like the perfect place to share with you something I like to call THE THREE TENETS OF EVAN. (Okay, that's a really hokey name, so if you can think of something better to call them, please e-mail me. Thanks.)

1. **Live Life Like You're Riding on a Wave.**
    Expect that good and bad experiences will flow in and out of your life. Sometimes the pitch of the wave will be steep and you'll have to really focus to stay on your feet. Sometimes you'll have the smoothest ride of your life. But you know that you are prepared for whatever comes. You are flexible and rooted firmly on your board. Emotions will ebb and flow like the tides. But as a spiritual warrior and a champion surfer, you are equipped with all the tools you need to combat negativity in your life. Remind yourself of this mantra: "Flexibility within stability." If you are confused about what that means, imagine a really tall, thin palm tree blowing in the wind. It bends and curves as the wind tosses it this way and that, but its roots stay firmly planted—it never falls.

Hero Pose (Virasana)

1. Kneel down on your knees and spread your feet apart so that your butt fits between them.
2. Place your hands on the floor. Inhale, then exhale and slowly lower your butt down to the ground.

Lying-Down Hero Pose (Supta Virasana)

1. Use your hands to lower yourself down so you can lie all the way back and down. (Try to keep your knees together and on the ground.)

2. **Keep an Open Heart.**
   Yogis say that we store all of our personal history in a space close to our hearts, called the solar plexus. The less we hold on to, the freer our hearts will be to let new experiences in. So it's important to practice opening the heart every single day.

Camel Pose (Ustrasana)

1. Place extra padding on the floor. You can double up your yoga mat.
2. Stand on your knees and tuck your butt under strongly. Press the tops of your feet into the ground so you are really using your thigh muscles.
3. Place your hands on your butt, fingers pointed down.
4. Inhale. Keep your chin tucked into your chest, shoulders relaxed.
5. Without crunching down on your lower back, arch your upper back as much as possible and lean back.
6. Breathe deeply, filling the heart with breath and prana.

7. **Advanced Camel:**
   Place your hands on the soles of your feet and drop your head and neck all the way back. Remember to keep lengthening your lower back.

Now do...

Child's Pose (Balasana)

1. Sit down on your heels.
2. Bring your head and chest
   down to the floor and your arms by your sides or straight out in
   front of you with your palms flat on the ground.

3. **Trust Your Intuition.**
   Believe in your innermost thoughts and listen to your inner voice.
   There is a secret part of you that just *knows*. Trust it. This is also the
   point from which you can distinguish what is true for you and what
   is just fear or fantasy.
      You can nurture this point by doing exercises to stimulate the
   sixth chakra, or your third eye. It is from this point that you can create the visions you want to manifest in your life.

••••••••PROJECTION MEDITATION

 Sit in Easy Pose, or if you're feeling extra talented, sit in Lotus Pose.

 Close your eyes and focus on the point between them, and slightly
   above, at your third eye point.

Picture your greatest wishes coming true. (Be sure to imagine everything in detail—the smell, the sounds, the feel....)

 Repeat your visions aloud or whisper them to yourself.

 Take ten deep breaths and envision the prana going directly into your visions and giving them life.

•••••••MANTRAS:

❋ I am in control of my emotions; my emotions are NOT in control of me.

❋ I believe in myself and have the courage to try new things.

❋ I let love flow in and out of me like a wave without becoming attached to things that are impermanent.

❋ I stand firmly planted on the earth—nothing can knock me over.

CHAPTER 7

The Perfectionist Girl

If God had wanted me otherwise, He would
have created me otherwise
— Johann Wolfgang von Goethe

Even though I've certainly blamed an annoying little brother or thighs I thought were too fat or an ex-boyfriend who broke my heart for my bad mood, I have found, more often than not, that the real source of pain comes from my own need to be perfect. It's as if many of us girls are born with an innate need to have the perfect beach body, be an academic genius, dance like Britney Spears, sing like Alicia Keys, win triathlons, and appear as a guest on late-night TV—all to prove to ourselves that we are worthwhile human beings. Thing is, everyone, movie stars and talk-show hosts included, has rough days. Of course it takes determination and concentration to work hard and accomplish our individual goals, but perfectionism certainly doesn't bring us fame or fortune or movie-star boyfriends. It only brings us down and prevents us from moving forward, messing up, and then learning from those mistakes.

When we strive for flawlessness, we lose our freedom to experiment. We are trying so hard to get everything we do exactly right that life stops being a fun, creative adventure. It's as if we're standing still, holding our breath, paralyzed for fear of failing. And the only time we do take a step forward is when we believe that it is a move toward perfection, when in reality it is a step toward an ideal and impossible vision of ourselves. When we believe that nothing we do or say is good enough, that we are defective in some way, we abandon the gifts and potential we were born with and we disclaim our truest selves.

For example, it took Katie until she was a junior in high school (and had been doing yoga for a year) to audition for her school play. All she ever wanted to do was be an actress, but since she had no experience at it, she figured it was a lost cause to even try. Oh my god, was she wrong! She is a natural. "Yeah," Katie shared, "it was like I knew I wasn't going to give a perfect performance since I'd never been in a play before, so I kept myself from even trying out for so long! Finally I realized that I needed to chill out and just give it a try— even if I did fail. And the thing is, I didn't fail at all! I got the lead!" But even if Katie hadn't gotten the lead, being bold enough to go for it would have been enough. She would still be a fabulous and courageous goddess girl, if not a fantastic actress.

I know that often it feels as if nothing we do, whether it's in school, sports, theater, or whatever, is good enough. Yeah, it's great to be disciplined and determined in our lives, but it's not okay to beat ourselves up for who we are, what we look like, or what we've yet to accomplish. The truth is, the reflection in the mirror is more about what we choose to see than what is really there. Sure, yoga can tone and strengthen your physical body, but its most profound work is what it does to your perception of yourself.

The more we celebrate who we are, with all our flaws and faults and eccentricities and individual talents, the more we will begin to feel, and I mean really feel, our own worth. On the other hand, the louder we call ourselves a failure and the more negative we are about our own intelligence, beauty, or performance, the less likely we are to succeed. This is because we create our world with our attitude and our projection. The world ultimately sees us as we see ourselves. And wouldn't it be an awesome feeling to love your mind and your body as much as you love Britney Spears'?

It's like in that Jon Mayer song "No Such Thing";
I don't want to stay "inside the lines," just because I'm supposed to.
I want to be MYSELF whether I'm considered perfect or not.
—Katie, age 17

YOGA POSTURES FOR THE "OH MY GOD I'M NOT PERFECT!" COMPLEX

Don't Suck It In! As girls in the twenty-first century, we're used to sucking in our stomachs, holding our breath so that we appear slimmer and taller. So it may feel unnatural and even uncomfortable to allow your tummy to expand outward, to intentionally let your belly relax and extend. Learning to do this, though, will enable you to have more energy, practice yoga more efficiently, and become as physically and mentally fit as you desire to be. To let go and surrender to the way your body is meant to be is a huge part of practicing yoga. Here are a series of postures that will help to loosen the tension we carry with us in our lower chakras that force us to look outside of ourselves for acceptance. These postures free that energy and allow us to begin to love the way we look and feel.

Sun Salutations (Surya Namaskara)

The sun salutations are probably the oldest, most widely practiced sequences of yoga positions. The people of India may not have had SPF 15 thousands of years ago, but they knew how good it felt to catch a few rays and, in doing so, pay their respect to the powerful benefits of the sun by honoring it through this sequence.

1. Stand with your feet shoulder-width apart. Bring your hands into prayer position at the center of your chest

2. Inhale and extend your arms up.

3. Exhale and bend at the waist, allowing your head and neck to fall gently.

4. Inhale and jump or step both legs back so that you are now in a push-up position, or Plank Pose.

5. Exhale and lower yourself down to the floor.

6. Inhale and slide yourself up into Cobra pose.*

Cobra (Bhujanga-asana): *Place your belly, legs, and tops of feet flat on the floor. Slide your hands and palms down 6–12 inches in front of your body and press your upper torso off the ground, keeping your elbows bent.*

7. Exhale and push yourself back into Downward-Facing Dog.

8. Inhale and step or jump your feet forward between your hands.
9. Exhale and let your body hang, bending at the waist.
10. Inhale and stand up, hands above your head in prayer position.

11. Exhale and gently bring your arms down, like wings, and return your hands to prayer position at the center of your chest.
12. Repeat anywhere from two to twenty times.

Sun salutations warm up your muscles, increase your flexibility, and stimulate the glands and organs of the entire body. If you aren't feeling too great, do a few sun salutes and that'll change. You can practice any of these postures individually, but when practiced in sequence, the postures should flow in synchronicity with the breath. (Sun salutations get you hot. And that's exactly how I'd describe you! So get movin'!)

MANTRAS:

- ❋ I am healthy and strong.
- ❋ My body, mind, and soul are in perfect harmony.
- ❋ I am grateful for every breath.
- ❋ I am the master of my physical body. My body does not control me.
- ❋ I am beautiful.

CHAPTER 8

Yoga and Your Body

There is but one temple in the universe, and that is the body.
— Novalis (1772-1801)

Several years ago, I did a summer yoga workshop with about thirty other girls, all led by an amazing teacher in Santa Monica, California. One of our exercises was to go around in a circle and describe how we were feeling about ourselves. I'll never forget what I said that day. At 5 feet 2 inches, and 110 pounds, I announced with tears in my eyes that I hated my body. Okay, now I have to admit, I was having a very emotional moment, I was totally PMS-ing, and I was assuming one of my favorite roles in life: drama queen. I didn't hate my body then and I don't hate it now, but I will tell you this: I must consciously make the choice to love my body each and every day. I choose to believe that I am perfect exactly as I am. 'Cause let's face it, girls—our bodies are one of the main things we try to get "perfect."

I took what I learned from my teacher and every so often have my students sit around in a circle, and we go around and talk about our feelings. The body pretty much wins out every month as the topic of choice for my girls. As I say in class, we girls need to band together and *redefine* what it means to have a "perfect" body. First and foremost, it means changing your perception of your own self. It means re-creating the image of yourself in your mind's eye, then projecting that and not some vision of "I'm so ugly" onto the world. The same eyes you use to admire surfer girls' bodies are the eyes with which you need to view yourself. When we stop beating ourselves up for who we are not, we allow ourselves the freedom to become who we truly are. And chances are, that person is a happy, beautiful girl of a healthy weight and size.

Instead of choosing to focus on what you think is wrong about yourself, why not try to celebrate the things you *like* about yourself? Think of it like this: if you take photos of ugly things, then your pictures are going to reflect that. But if you take pictures of beautiful images, that's what people will see. Same with mental pictures. How you see yourself is how others will see you. And what better way to learn self-acceptance than to see yourself as absolutely fantastic!

What we think, we become.
—Buddha

It's kind of hard to believe that our thoughts, those little, silent vibrations in our brains, can actually affect reality, but it's true. What we think becomes our reality. I don't mean to say that if you think you're fat, then you become fat. But rather, if you put lots of energy into a false belief, you give life to it and soon you live your life as if it were true. Or maybe you'll better understand it like this: If a famous singer like, say, Hilary Duff told herself that she was somehow tragically flawed and she truly believed this in her mind, then every other aspect of her life would be somehow affected by this negative self-image. She might never put herself out there and sing her songs in public. Hollywood would never have discovered her, and she would never have achieved all of her musical accomplishments. Yes, she is beautiful. But she must know this in order for everyone else to see it too.

Has someone ever told you not to think too highly of yourself? Well, I'm here to say you go right ahead and think the world of yourself. Now I'm not saying to jump on your high horse and look down upon all the little people you stumble across at the mall. I'm not encouraging you to become an egomaniac. Instead, I want you to think of yourself as the most beautiful, wise, and worthy version of yourself. I just happen to believe that a *little bit* of conceit and a *whole lotta* self-lovin' is necessary in our day and age for a girl to know how gorgeous she really is!

By shaping your perception of yourself, you unconsciously shape others' perceptions of you as well. It's the coolest thing — the mirror effect. The outer world is like a mirror that reflects your inner world. Be nice to yourself and the world will be nice back. Love yourself and the world will love you back. I know a few of you girls are just rolling your eyes at me right now, wishing it were only so easy to just love yourself. No, it's not easy, but it can be done. And yoga will help you get there.

You see, when you break a sweat in yoga, you're not only freeing physical toxins from deep in your muscles, but you're also releasing negative beliefs stored in the body. Yoga requires you to connect to each part of your body and to feed breath into places you usually cram with insults. Yoga demands that you remind yourself, over and over again, how truly great you are.

·········TELL YOUR INNER CRITIC TO TAKE A HIKE!

If you are an athlete and you want to win a game, what do you do right before the game? You amp yourself up, tell yourself and your teammates that you rock, that this game is yours. Or if you are getting ready for the homecoming dance, do you take your brand-new dress, throw it on the floor, and stomp all over it before you put it on? Of course not! So then why do we tell ourselves how horrible we are, how fat or ugly or stupid or insignificant we are, when all we really want to be is the very best? Doesn't make much sense, does it?

Positive change starts with you. Sure, there's always the occasional "extreme makeover," but first, let's just get a few things straight in our heads: your negative self-talk is not helping you to get anywhere. In fact, it's actually like a roadblock keeping you from going to the party of all parties! And I know if someone were to stand in my way, I'd tell them to move over, 'cause I've got somewhere to be. That's exactly what I want you to do to your inner critic. Tell her to get the heck out of your way! I want you to rebel! I want you to defy what she has to say. If she tells you you're too fat, you tell her differently. If she tells you that you will surely fail, you remind her, one by one, of all of your successes. Then tell her that that list is only the beginning! You can go right ahead and say to that inner enemy: "I am learning to eat better, I practice yoga, and I know that my body is perfect exactly as it is in this moment!"

Corny as it sounds, it is the era of self-acceptance, girls. I know it can be tough at first to really accept ourselves, but each of us girls must learn to get butt naked, stand in front of a mirror, and celebrate the beautiful beings that we are. As I said earlier, loving your body is a *choice*. And guess what? You get to choose! Yoga makes this choice simple: you feel so good in your own skin that you couldn't imagine living in anyone else's. Renee, a student and friend, is a perfect example. As she said herself:

When I was doing yoga, I felt my body become longer, leaner...

I just felt better. I felt happier with how I looked. And I never thought it could happen, but I really don't hate my body anymore. I mean, I have my days, but I get over it. But it wasn't until I stopped doing yoga for a few weeks that I really noticed the difference it made in my body. I look back and realize how much stronger I feel. The real difference it made was on the inside, though. I feel braver now. I'm a lot less moody and self-critical. I feel good, so I don't tend to be extra critical of every part of my body now.

In today's world, it's nearly impossible not to question our bodies at some point. But that's okay. We just need to work that much harder to love ourselves. Renee did it. I do it every single day. And so can you.

········ Yoga for a Positive Body Image

Seated Forward Bend (Paschimottanasana)

This asana balances the first three chakras, or our "lower triangle," which leads to self-acceptance and a feeling of being grounded and confident. It also has a calming effect on the body.

1. Sit on the floor with your legs stretched out in front of you, about hip-width apart.

2. Inhale and sit up really straight, and reach your arms up above your head so your elbows are near your ears.

3. Exhale, fold forward, and reach your hands down the length of your legs as far as you can, without going into pain territory.

4. Breathe long and deep as you stretch farther forward and down.

One-Legged Forward Bend (Janusirasana)

This pose opens up the pathways of energy in your body and frees up your inner girl power, or "shakti."

1. Sit on the floor with your left leg stretched out in front of you and your right foot bent alongside your left thigh.
2. Inhale, arms up.
3. Exhale, and fold forward. (Do not push the stretch. Keep your knees slightly bent until you develop your flexibility.)
4. Take five long, deep breaths here.

5. Change sides so your right leg is stretched out in front and your left foot is bent alongside your right thigh. Repeat.

From here, lie down flat on your back for some ab asanas!

Basic Abs or "Yogic Sit-ups"

Whenever we work our abdominals, we activate our third chakra, which is our power center. These poses relate to fear of rejection, how we look, and how we think others see us. Ab work helps us to empower ourselves through strengthening our "core," or the center of our beings.

1. Lie flat on your back, hands behind the base of your head.
2. Raise your legs, knees bent, up into the air, and flex your feet.
3. Inhale, and lift your tailbone off the ground.
4. Hold the breath.
5. Exhale, and lift your head and chest, crunching toward your legs.
6. Inhale, and lay back down. Keep your feet raised in the air.
7. Repeat five to ten times. Increase number of yogic sit-ups gradually.

Ultimate Core Balance (Navasana)

This is one of my favorite ab asanas because it gives you such a sense of accomplishment when you get it. Navasana will make you feel stronger, more focused, and best of all, in control of your own life.

1. Sit on your butt with your legs extended in front of you.
2. Lean back slightly, placing your weight onto your hands, and lift your legs up in the air to about 60 degrees.
3. Suck your tummy in, tilt your pelvis in, and lift your chest up.
4. Inhale, and slowly bring your hands off the ground and stretch them out in front of you.
5. Breathe as you use your core to balance in this pose.

Be sure to practice patience and self-compassion as you work on achieving this pose.

❈ I live in the perfect body for my spirit.
❈ I am beautiful on the inside and out.
❈ I treat my body with love, respect, and compassion.
❈ My body is strong, healthy, and hot!

FYI: GOOD VIBRATIONS!

Did you know that the smallest existing particles are actually just vibrating pieces of matter? That means that on one level or another, the whole universe is made of sound. Look at the word "universe." When you break it down, UNI means "one" and VERSE means "word." So even just ONE WORD can change the whole vibration of your existence. And you get to *choose* which words you use to speak to yourself. You can create good vibrations!

CHAPTER 9

Diet and Nutrition

Let your food be your medicine.
— Hippocrates

Okay, so you want to feel your best *and* have a rockin' bod, right? Well, you can't do that if you're starving yourself or if you're pounding candy bars like Willy Wonka is going out of business. Neither extreme will cut it. Balance is key when it comes to food. And yoga can help you find balance in more than just your handstand. It will help you to steady your appetite and change the way you look at food for the better.

Have a seat, grab a blended café mocha, and allow me to introduce you to an awesome girl who swore she was doomed to a lifetime of carrot sticks and water. Meet Molly. I love Molly because I was a lot like her when I was fifteen—poised and confident on the outside, but really kind of bummed out on the inside. Somewhere along the line, Molly heard from a few mean kids in elementary school that she was on the chubby side. So when she got to junior high, she started working out like a madwoman. Her weight normalized just as she was hitting puberty and then, well, things started to fill out. Still, Molly was as fit and toned as a girl could aspire to be. Even the boys who used to tease her now admired her attractive and super-fit body.

Problem was, Molly still thought of herself as the chubby little girl in fourth grade. So in her effort to become as skinny as she could be, she worked very hard at limiting what she ate. Every calorie of every meal was perfectly planned out. Even when Molly wasn't consciously thinking about food, she was thinking about food (probably because she was so darn hungry after all the working out she did!). I vividly remember when I first talked to Molly about her issues with food, she recalled how upset she was that she had eaten "sooo much" that day, including "five licorice ropes, two graham crackers, eight M&Ms," and so on. She must have burned off a hundred calories just doing that kind of math!

I could totally relate to Molly's struggles, so I knew that if she was up for doing some yoga, then she would have a chance at having a better relationship with food. She didn't know anyone when she first came to my yoga class. I knew it took some guts to show up alone, and I was fully impressed with her for coming—and we hadn't even begun the yoga yet! But Molly didn't see the same girl the rest of us saw when she looked in the mirror. In fact, she hated the girl she saw. And the way Molly dealt with feelings of low self-esteem was by strictly controlling what she ate. It made her feel good about herself to have such self-control. And while I've never known a girl who, at least at one point or another, didn't face concerns about her weight or size, I knew a girl on her way to an eating disorder when I saw one.

Although her food troubles and anxiety over her weight didn't just instantly disappear, Molly started to feel a lot better about herself as she focused more of her attention on being a healthy and happy girl and less time on how unlucky and unhappy she was. She began to realize that, in order to have enough energy to get through the day, and then get through a yoga class, she needed to give her body the proper fuel. Molly also started seeing herself more clearly. That is, instead of imagining herself as an ugly duckling, she started seeing herself, physically looking in the mirror and seeing herself, as beautiful.

•••••• WEIGHT A MINUTE, EAT HEALTHY

It seems that most girls are pretty hung up on food. Lately, there seems to be this notion floating around that the thinner we are, the better we are. And girls, this simply is not true. Nonetheless, I think it's pretty safe to say that many of us girls have perfected the ultimate love/hate relationship with food. I can't even remember a time when we weren't bombarded by our culture's obsession with being thin. All of a sudden, we've gone from munching on a slice of pizza and sipping a soda for lunch to counting the calories in two carrot sticks, a bowl of lettuce, and a tablespoon of fat-free salad dressing. Somewhere along the line we collectively decided that "eating healthfully" means, well, barely eating at all.

Sometimes you just have to stop what you're doing, put down the phone, drop the nail file, and reassess your life. Okay, so maybe not your whole entire life, but how you are feeding and nourishing your body. Are you eating healthy foods? Or are you more concerned with how eating will make you look than how it will make you *feel*? Could you have fallen into the "food-friend trap?" Okay, so this isn't an official thing. It's a term I made up to describe the phenomenon of how easily influenced we are by the diets of our friends.

Everyone has a different body and different needs, but we compare ourselves to our friends and think we need to be exactly like them in order to be accepted. We look at every part of their bodies and think, "Gosh, my butt should be that small" or, "I wish my figure looked as good as hers" and stuff like that. We say ridiculous things to ourselves like, "She's so thin, she must not have a single problem! I wish I were her." We watch what they eat, and if everyone is eating cheeseburgers, then we think, "Okay, I'll have one too." But if everyone is eating salad, then you think, "I'd better only have a salad. Dressing on the side."

It's a very common phenomenon. Like on TV shows, you might notice one of the actresses becomes really thin, then before you know it, all the actresses on the same show are thinner. We girls have this amazing ability to unify with one another. But sometimes uniting becomes conforming, and often, that conforming does more than hurt your individual spirit—it can wreak havoc on your health.

There is no one way to eat, no one way to be healthy, and no one right answer to our personal questions about food and how to deal with the pressures we face. All we can do is be there for one another, support one another, help ourselves to have a healthy relationship with food. Yoga helps us to do this on so many levels. It brings us together as a group. It encourages us to listen to what our bodies need to be healthy and strong. It also works on levels we aren't even aware of, like on chemical and biological levels. Practicing yoga regularly automatically balances your appetite. When we nourish ourselves from the inside out, as we do in yoga, we learn to eat only if we are hungry and to take a step back if we are just trying to fill an empty space inside ourselves.

SPECIAL YOGA FOR CHIPS AND COOKIES: PREVENTING YOUR CRAVINGS FROM GETTING THE BEST OF YOU

One of the best yoga exercises I do to get in touch with whether I am truly hungry or am just eating to fill a void is a special version of abdominal crunches (explained at the end of this chapter). These immediately get you in touch with your belly. With Molly, I knew that, first and foremost, she needed to learn to accept and love her body exactly as it was in the "now" moment. In order to do that, I needed to teach her to feel her belly—not with her hands, but from the inside out. This way, she'd be more in touch with when she was hungry, and she'd be more likely to honor what her body was telling her with nutritious foods. Getting in touch with her belly or her third chakra, the power center, would also enable Molly to feel more self-control so that she would know if she was eating out of stress or sadness or any purpose other than hunger. Slowly but surely, Molly began to discover a sense of peace about her body. It was really amazing to watch because it just reaffirmed what I already knew to be true: that practicing yoga can remedy even the wildest of hang-ups.

I think it's time we stood up and took responsibility for our own decisions about food and body image. ('Cause, girls, the world ain't gonna change for us. We've got to make it happen.) Although we may see pictures of models pasted on every billboard from Los Angeles to Kalamazoo (and beyond!), it is up to us to take charge of how we eat, what we eat, and most of all, how we respond to images on the cover of *Cosmo*.

·········· YOU ARE WHAT YOU EAT (ANNOYING, BUT TRUE!)

Eating healthfully is less about attaining a body like a supermodel's and more about self-esteem. When we like ourselves, when we recognize that we deserve to be healthy, happy, and strong, then we tend to make decisions that will help us, not hurt us. On the other hand, if we believe our lives are insignificant or we practice self-hatred, then we're more likely to make unhealthy choices. More simply, when we like ourselves, we choose to eat foods that make us feel good. Some of you aren't even concerned about your diet; you are healthy and strong and eat what you want. Then there are some of you who struggle with losing weight, and eating properly is more of a challenge for you than for others. That's okay too. Eating healthfully is a lifetime endeavor for all of us girls. It is important for all of us to eat foods that nourish our bodies and souls, that give us energy to be the healthiest and happiest girls we can possibly be. If you are what you eat, then it's important to choose wisely. And this book can help you do that.

FYI: SHOULD I BECOME A VEGETARIAN?

Although many yogis are also vegetarians, you do not have to go 100 percent veggie if it's not your thing. I've spoken to several doctors, and they have all told me that neither option is healthier than the other, that it's completely a personal decision. Dr. Martin Cooper, a big, fancy doctor in Beverly Hills, even told me, "Evan, whether you choose to go vegetarian or not, as long as you get sufficient protein and the nutrients you need, then you will be a healthy young lady." (By the way, beans, nuts, tofu, soy, and cheese are all especially good sources of protein for vegetarians.)

Ray of Light Twist
(Marichyasana)

Twisting poses help to stimulate digestion and act as a detoxifier for our bodies. Twists have an amazing ability to create balance in our appetites, as well as in our relationship with what we put into our bodies.

1. Sit on the floor with your left leg extended out in front of you and your right knee bent, the right foot flat on the floor next to your left inner thigh.
2. Place your right hand on the floor next to you for balance.
3. Place your left elbow against the outside of your right knee, keeping your hand in the air and your thumb and index finger touching in "gyan mudra."
4. Inhale, lift your chest, and roll your shoulders back.
5. Exhale, and twist your torso to the right.
6. Take three breaths here. Then switch sides.

Crisscross Abs

(More yogic sit-ups!)

1. Lie on your back and clasp your hands behind your head. Lift your legs with bent knees.
2. Inhale, and curl your head and chest up.
3. Hold the breath. Lift your tailbone off the ground.
4. Exhale. Cross your right elbow to your left knee.
5. Inhale and come back to center.
6. Repeat and cross your left elbow to your right knee.
7. Continue for several rounds.

These yoga postures stimulate your body to release endorphins in the blood and serotonin in the brain—these are feel-good chemicals that help balance your appetite. Your body literally readjusts itself so that you only give it what it needs. And when you aren't obsessing over what to eat and when, then you can start to focus more on the things that matter—like what a hot babe you are!

❁ Eating junk will make me feel like junk. Eating whole, natural foods will make me feel energetic and beautiful.

❁ I have a healthy, balanced appetite.

❁ I eat foods that nourish my body.

❁ I eat foods that nurture my soul.

❁ I trust my body to tell me what it needs.

CHAPTER 10

From Girl 2 Goddess

You must be the change you want to see in the world.
— Mahatma Gandhi

BARBIE DOESN'T GET HER PERIOD, WHY DO I HAVE TO?

Christina was one of my regular yoga girls, so when she stopped showing up for class out of nowhere, I decided to shoot her an e-mail. No response. So then I gave her a call. First, I was making sure she was still alive and breathing. Then I was calling to find out why she hadn't gotten her butt to yoga in over a month. I never expected her to tell me that she no longer felt comfortable doing yoga with the other girls, and that her mom had bought her a yoga DVD that she was doing at home, alone. I was like, "Christina, what's the deal? You love your friends! You love coming to yoga! What changed?"

"I feel gross. I hate my body."

Well, I knew this was just not typical of Christina. Stressed out from school? Sure. Boy problems? All the time. Issues with her body? Never.

91

Something had changed, something was bothering her.

So I took a risk and asked if anything had happened. I was honest and just told her that I could feel that something was different and maybe it would help to share it with someone she trusted.

After a brief pause, Christina softly answered, "I got my period."

And then she got real quiet, which was probably because she felt somewhat embarrassed about sharing this very personal news. I was quick to reassure her that it was cool to be kind of uneasy about it, since I have distinct memories of being fourteen and going through this myself.

"Ahhh…okay, now I get it. Say no more. But will you have lunch with me one day so we can catch up, talk about the things that are bothering you?"

And then such an enthusiastic burst of energy followed I was almost blown over through the phone. "You mean without anyone else? Just you and me? Totally! That would be awesome. I would love that."

Ah, now that was typical Christina!

Getting your period is by far one of the strangest, most uncomfortable phenomena of growing up. All of a sudden, you have to deal with a week of feeling crampy, moody, bloated, and PMS-y, followed by a week of cramming tampons in every pocket and purse you own just to make sure you're covered. Your body feels weird. It's like, what the heck is happening to me? When I got my period, I swore to my parents that it wasn't normal and that I was dying. Honestly, I really thought I was dying—even though I knew it was about time for me to get my period.

Christina was frightened too. But more than being afraid for her physical life, she was afraid for her social life. None of her other friends had gone through this yet, and she had yet to discover all the incredible aspects of no longer being a "little" girl. That's why I met her for lunch. I didn't want her to stop doing the things she loved simply because she was growing up. I wanted her to know how fun it can be to be a full-fledged teenager! She's back in class now, so I think it worked.

CHANGES IN BODY AND SOUL

I like to think of adolescence as the journey from girl to goddess. Being a teen is more than just the time that you grow boobs and get your period—it's the time when you go from a caterpillar, sheltered by the cocoon of your parents' love, to a brilliant butterfly, who can soar through life on her own terms. It is a slow process but an exciting one, because you start to understand things in a way you never did before. You put down the dolls and start looking in the mirror at your-self, examining the changes you see occurring and becoming curious about what the future holds.

I know, your boobs hurt.

You weigh, like, ten pounds more than you did a year ago. (Where did these hips come from?)

You're finally "allowed" to date boys, but no one is asking!

And the one person who you used to tell everything to (aka Mom) hasn't got a clue!

What the heck is going on?

Although the teen transition is often a rocky road, it is a path lined with beautiful wildflowers—and they're yours for the picking. Okay, so that's kind of a corny analogy, but just work with me here. Some of these great flowers are those of the spirit (courage, strength, freedom), and some are of the physical world (high heels, dating, driving). I think when I was a teen, I was so wrapped up in the drama and discomfort of it all, I didn't realize how much fun I was really having. Of course, when you're PMS-ing or "Cousin Flo" is in town, I totally get it that you might not feel like throwing a "Yay, I'm a woman now" party! That's why I'm going to give you some yoga postures to practice for those times when you'd rather just trade in your *Vogue* magazine and go back to watching *SpongeBob*.

PMS AND YOUR MOON CYCLE

As females, we're all going to have to deal with crazy hormonal changes at some point or another. So why not do it gracefully? All right, so maybe dealing with getting your period gracefully is a little too much to ask, since all too often, you'll experience sore boobs, mad chocolate cravings, and the occasional "Uh-oh, does anyone have a tampon?" But it doesn't hurt to at least understand what's going on with your body and then know how to make it feel a little better.

One day, before we started class, everyone was all hyped up. I mean, it was mayhem in the yoga room. I swear ten different conversations must have been happening at one time! Somehow, I overheard one of my students announce to the rest of the girls, "Having your period is a pain in the ass!" I decided to jump into the conversation at this point. I said something along the lines of what I'm about to tell you.

Okay, so having my period is not my first choice for a good time, but it can also be a really beautiful, personal time for a girl. It's a time when some pretty amazing things are happening in your body, if you think about it. (It's also a great excuse to take a day off from that mandatory swim class you've got in PE!) Thing is, we're so uncomfortable talking about it, which doesn't really make sense, since we're all going to go through it.

Personally, I think we should get over it, have a revolution of girl talk, and discuss away! I think speaking about our bodies the way the yogis do could help, because in India, sexuality has beautiful symbolic meaning.

In yogic terms, female energy is related to the moon, and male energy to the sun. Our periods are directly affected by the force of the moon (the word "menses" means moons!). This means that, during this time of the month, we can balance out our crazy emotions, raging hormones, and feeling like we weigh as much as an elephant by focusing on what we need: sun energy. This is one of the best times to practice your sun salutations. When you have your period, or when you're in your "moon cycle," yoga can help you tap into what your body needs. Does it need sun energy? Does it need a nap? Or does it need a bite of chocolate ice cream? Doing yoga, becoming silent and still, can help you hear what your body is saying to you. Most importantly, it can help you turn off the tears and feel like your normal self again.

Yoga for PMS

Sun Salutations (see chapter 7)
Crisscross Abs (see chapter 9)

Happy Baby Pose

This is one of my girls' favorite poses, and once you try it, you'll see why. It can soothe nervous energy, tummy aches, and cramps like you wouldn't believe!

1. Lie on your back, lift your legs in the air, and grab the outer soles of your feet. (Obviously, you'll have to bend your knees to do this.)
2. Gently pull your legs down toward your chest.
3. Take several long, deep breaths into your belly.

Legs on the Wall (version of Urdhava Prasarita Padasana)

Another great one to ease cramps and bring relief to a restless body and mind.

1. Sit down near a wall, and scoot your butt up close to it.
2. Lie down on the ground and place your legs straight up onto the wall.
3. Place your hands flat on the ground and breathe deeply, feeding breath into your organs.

You can practice the following poses individually or in a flowing sequence (described below), which I find especially soothing during this time of the month.

Mountain Pose (Tadasana)

1. Stand up tall and straight.
2. Roll your shoulders back.
3. Tuck your tailbone down (in other words, don't let your butt stick out).
4. Imagine a silver cord coming down from the sky, straight down through the top of your head, down the length of your body, and through your feet into the ground.
5. Breathe.

Standing Forward Bend (Uttanasana)

1. Stand in Mountain Pose.
2. Inhale, and reach your hands up above your head.
3. Exhale, release your arms down, and fold forward from the waist.
4. Bring your hands onto the floor, keeping your knees

slightly bent until you feel flexible enough to straighten them.

5. Breathe.

Sequence:

Practice coordinating your breath and movement so they flow together like a dance. On particularly bloated, icky-feeling days, this sequence can give you a feeling of lightness, ease, and grace.

1. Inhale, and stand in Mountain Pose.
2. Exhale, and fold down into Standing Forward Bend.
3. Inhale, and with a flat back, lift your head and chest. Your hands come up onto your shins.
4. Exhale, and fold into Standing Forward Bend.
5. Inhale, and spiral the arms up toward the sky as you stand up into Mountain Pose again.
6. Exhale, and release your hands down into prayer position at the center of your chest.

Downward-Facing Dog (Adho Mukha Savasana)
(see chapter 5)

Child's Pose (Balasana)
(see chapter 6)

During your period, many yoga experts recommend giving the belly a rest and not doing any abdominal exercises. Other teachers say do *more* abs during this time of the month. You need to do what feels best for your own body. For me, personally, doing a few light ab exercises helps me because they stimulate the blood and get things flowing, so I have fewer cramps.

There is always one true inner voice. Trust it.
—Gloria Steinem, REVOLUTION FROM WITHIN

········ WHAT IT MEANS TO BE A GODDESS

To be able to trust your own inner voice is the number one characteristic of a true goddess. It means self-reliance and self-appreciation. It means knowing that you are strong enough to handle whatever comes your way. It means that if you had nothing but your li'l old self, you'd be okay. No, you'd be more than okay. Becoming a goddess means more than simply leaving childhood for adulthood. It means overcoming your biggest fears. It means making friends with your demons. It means charting your own course when the world tells you to play it safe. If everyone spoke the same way, wore the same clothes, and thought the same thing, life would be so boring. I want you to be the color of your world when everyone else is wearing black and white. You don't literally have to wear pink polka dots to be your own person. All you have to do is walk the path that is right for you. Rebel against the norm. Use what's in *you* to be great, rather than conforming to everyone else to be mediocre.

> What lies behind us and what lies before us are tiny matters compared to what lies within us.
> —Ralph Waldo Emerson

·······WHAT'S SHAKTI GIRL?

So what exactly is it that we each have within ourselves? We have the power of creation or, in yogic terms, Shakti.

I was sitting around with a few of my girls one day after class, and one of them mentioned that she was frustrated because, as she said, "You could talk self-help mumbo jumbo for eternity and it still won't make your problems go away!" Well, she's right. "Self-help" talk doesn't work magic. But we finally all agreed that yoga was the best thing they'd discovered up until now to help them deal. And that's pretty magical. So why *does* yoga work so well? Because everything you do when you practice yoga—from the physical asanas to the mental focus required to chanting your heart out—brings you more in touch with your inner girl power. And in yoga, this female power is known as Shakti.

Actually, Shakti is the name of an ancient Indian goddess who represents the power of creation and the ever-changing, flowing, dynamic aspect of ourselves. She is the embodiment of "flexibility within stability." Shakti, however, cannot be mentioned without talking about the god Shiva, her male counterpart, who signifies the stable, unchanging aspect of life. Together, Shiva and Shakti represent the power within every man and woman, every god and goddess. Without Shakti, however, Shiva is nothing. He needs his Shakti girl! And each and every girl has this Shakti power within herself. All you have to do is remind yourself to tap into it. Your power to create *anything you dream to create* never leaves you, no matter how down you may get, no matter how much you disbelieve in yourself. You are always a Shakti girl. You just need to know it!

·········GODDESS POSES

Straddle Abs

In order to fully embrace your Shakti, it's important to get in touch with the parts of you that are uniquely feminine, 'cause this is where all that power resides. Straddle Abs really gets you in touch with your second and third chakras: your centers of creation and power!

1. Lay down on your back and bring your legs into a wide straddle position, feet flexed back.
2. Place both hands on your lower belly or straight ahead and press down with a little bit of pressure.
3. Inhale, and lift your head, neck, and chest off the ground.
4. Exhale, and curl your tailbone and hips up and into your hands.
5. Repeat several times.

Note: Before you do the following poses, I recommend warming up and doing Bridge Pose first. [see chapter 4]

Scorpion Variation Pose (variation of Caravakasana)

Back bends are a great goddess pose because there is something really graceful that radiates through your body when you open your heart, like you do in back bends. Scorpion Variation is one I *like to practice in preparation for my personal favorite goddess pose: Dancer.*

1. Sit on all fours, your hands and knees hip-distance apart.
2. Reach back and grab the inside of your left foot with your left hand.
3. Breathe deep Ujjayi breaths.
4. Relax down. Change sides.

Dancer

Dancer is both a back bend and a balancing pose. When you are able to simultaneously discover the balance and gracefulness in your body, your mind and spirit have no choice but to follow. Dancer teaches you patience and courage, and it rewards you with a taste of your own divinity.

1. Stand up.
2. Find your balance on your right foot, and reach your right hand straight out in front of you.
3. Grab the inside of your left foot with your left hand.

4. As you find your balance, slowly begin to lift the left leg up and back as you lean forward and reach out through your right hand.

5. Choose a spot about four feet in front of you and focus your gaze on it as you come deeper into the pose. Breathe.

Note: This is an advanced pose. Take your time. Recognize your frustration as a passing emotion. Then breathe. And try again.

Abs, Again!

Choose any abdominal exercise. After back bends, which is what we are doing in Scorpion Variation and Dancer, it is vital to relieve any strain in the back. Abs are the best way to do this.

CHAPTER 11

Yoga and Relationships

I've learned a lot from my new relationship. I've
learned that the only way I could enjoy being with my
boyfriend was to learn how to enjoy being without him.
I had to learn to love myself as much as I loved him.
— Stephanie Klempner, yogini and friend extraordinaire

According to classic yogic philosophy, we're not supposed to get too attached to anyone or anything. The principle of "non-attachment" to people, places, and all things in the material world is a big one for yogis. But let's just get real: it's almost impossible to accomplish this when the thing you are attached to is a guy. The reality is, we do fasten ourselves onto the things around us and in our lives, no matter how hard we may try to warn ourselves about the potential for disappointment. If we are meant to give ourselves fully to life, to experience every opportunity given to us, then we have to take risks in what we do and whom we love. And of course that risk includes becoming attached to someone who may not love us back. For this reason, I have found that lessons of non-attachment are particularly challenging when it comes to dating.

Sometimes our affection for a guy will be reciprocated with an invitation to the prom or a stolen kiss at the end of movie night with the gang. Other times, the guy you like may be too caught up in his own world, in football practice, in his rock band, in another girl, to return the love you so undeniably deserve. (No, this is not the time when I tell you that it's okay to super-glue his locker shut.) But you can turn to your yoga practice and to your faith in the universe's plan for you, which most certainly includes a hot date at some point or another. Learning to let go of your attachment to others includes allowing yourself to feel pain. It is normal to feel let down and sad, and you should not deny that these feelings exist. But once you have, it's time to reach for the love you are missing from the person you know best: *yourself.*

••••••••FIRST DATES AND THE ONES THAT FOLLOW...

Personally, I can think of nothing more exciting or terrifying than a first date, especially when the date is with someone you already have a mad crush on. I mean, could your heart beat any faster if you were skydiving? I don't think so! Before I became a full-time yoga instructor, I worked at a magazine where I interviewed celebrities and rock stars.

At that time, I can remember pleading with my boss, the editor of the magazine, to set me up with a very hot, semifamous musician. I knew that the date would probably never really happen and I convinced myself that any attempt to win a date with, let's just call him Jack, was solely an attempt to entertain my wandering mind and restless heart.

Well, we did set up a date and the prospect of meeting Jack was so exciting that I could barely concentrate on my work. My heart beat fast and my breathing was rapid and shallow. So as soon as I got home from work, I immediately sat down to do some "first-date yoga." My hair could look good, I might have the perfect pair of hipster jeans huggin' my behind, but if my sense of mental and spiritual balance was off, I'd be sure to trip and fall, stutter and slur. So clearing my mind was the most important preparation I could do before I met this hottie.

DATING, WAITING BY THE PHONE, AND THE WOES OF BEING WOOED

When feelings of self-doubt arise, I sit down on my fluffy rug reserved for meditation and revisit the only thing that is certain: my spirit. I've learned that if I am going to feel a sense of peace about dating, guys coming in and out of my life, and all the feelings that come with it, then I have to be the one in charge of my attitude and state of mind. Yoga enables us to do this. Yoga is a mental discipline as well as a physical one, and its philosophies teach us how incredibly helpful a simple shift in attitude can be to our lives. Of course, in cases such as dating cute boys, a single meditation may not be enough to make us feel okay about the whole situation.

We might have to practice what I call "meditation in action." By this, I simply mean that in every moment, I remind myself to inhale and exhale deeply, to pull my shoulders down and back, to continue to bring my mind back to the present moment and to the task at hand when it starts to wander or feel sad. It means reminding myself that I am the master of my thoughts and feelings, and that if I want to be okay with my situation, it is in my power to make it be okay. "Meditation in action" is living each minute as it comes to me without fear, without hesitation, with only the thought of my own greatness and beauty in mind.

My friend Jessie has learned similar lessons in the land of love. Jessie and I have spent many an afternoon, post-yoga class, chatting about boys and all the pain they can cause if we let them. So one afternoon, we made a pact (which you can do with one of your friends too). We vowed to always trust our own hearts and only do what feels right to us. Also, we vowed never to do anything we're uncomfortable with just because we think it will make a boy like us more.

The summer before Jessie came to my yoga class, she had just learned a great lesson in trusting herself. I'll let her tell you just as she told the story to me.

Two summers ago, I was in love with this guy at summer camp named Josh. I truly considered dating him to be a fantasy because Josh was "the" guy at camp—the cute, fun guy that every girl wanted to be with. I just thought, as great as it would be, he would never pick me. He probably had no idea who I was.

Well, on the first day back at camp the next summer, I realized he knew who I was when he struck up a conversation with me. The second night of camp, I found out that he'd been asking around about me. The fourth night of camp, we had our first kiss. I dated Josh for one great month (which, in camp terms, feels like a year). Anyway, we had a great time together, laughing and hanging out.

Well, Josh was also one of my first boyfriends, and I didn't know that much about relationships. I was very worried that I was going to do something to mess it up, so instead of just trusting my instincts, I tried to follow the advice of my more "experienced" friends. Unfortunately, I was also naive enough to follow what I thought was friendly advice from one of his friends. His friend told me, in confidence, that Josh was disappointed with our relationship because it wasn't physical enough. So I started cutting short conversations—interesting conversations that he would start about problems he was having as a counselor or poetry he was interested in—to hook up with him. About a week and a half later, Josh broke up with me, telling me he didn't think we had the right balance between talking and being physical. He said that, after one month, we talked so little he still didn't feel like he knew me that well.

Needless to say, I was devastated. I was also too much in shock to try to explain to him what I was doing (that is, doing what I thought he wanted). So we never got back together. We eventually became friends, but I've always regretted not letting that relationship develop the way I thought it should and instead trying to force things to happen the way other people told me they should.

Talk about learning a lesson in living life according to your own heart! We have to do what feels right to us. And doing what's right for us, more often than not, works out! It's like this: when you go against what you feel in your gut is right for you, it's like swimming upstream rather than going with the natural flow of things. The only way you'll ever get where you want to be in life is to remain true to *yourself.*

Rather than hang on to the affection of a boy to make ourselves feel good, we can give this love and support to ourselves instantly, constantly, the moment we need it and even when we don't. Yoga helps us to do this. The exercises give us the strength to stand up for what we believe in, and yogic philosophy teaches us how to soothe our souls when nothing else will.

FYI: PRESCRIPTION FOR AN OPEN HEART

Do Yoga

In Sanskrit, the fourth chakra, the heart chakra, is known as *anahata,* which means "unstuck." Yoga, practiced regularly over a period of time, has this incredible ability to open up your heart in ways you never imagined possible. In any given yoga class, you may see people crying quietly or laughing hysterically—that's yoga freeing their hearts of anything that was hidden or stuck inside. When your heart opens, it's like a huge relief because all of the pain that has ever struck your heart fades into forgiveness and all the love you experience is free to flow in and out. Nothing gets stuck; you just feel free to love and be loved.

YOGA FOR DEALING WITH THE BOYS

Prayer Squats (Malasana)

Prayer Squats are a very grounding exercise. They stimulate your first chakra, which helps you feel strong, grounded, and rooted in your own individual strength and beauty.

1. Stand with your feet hip-width apart, hands at the center of your

chest in prayer position.

2. Inhale, and lift your hands above your head, bringing your palms together.

3. Exhale. Slowly lower yourself down to a squatting position.

4. Inhale, and return to standing; exhale, squat. Continue for several rounds.

Seated Straddle Pose (Upavistha Konasana)

A hip opener, Seated Straddle Pose will help to bring balance to your first and second chakras, the energy centers where our need for acceptance can be fulfilled. This pose helps to ground you to the earth, helping you to feel safe, secure, and rested.

1. Sit with your legs spread out in a V before you.

2. Straighten your legs and flex your feet.

3. Slowly walk your hands out until your body is resting comfortably on the floor. (You may need to bring your legs closer together. That's okay.)

4. Breathe long and deep.

Okay, so as much as they drive us crazy, it's true, we love the boys (unless we don't, and that's okay too!). Even the original goddess of girl power, Shakti, had a divine male counterpart, Shiva. Together, they created the balance necessary in the universe. Whereas Shakti is the creative power, Shiva is the destructive force. (You can't rebuild if you don't first tear down, right?) So listen up, all you Shakti girls out there: have faith, 'cause one day your perfect Shiva boy will come along!

CHAPTER 12

Gettin' Along with Family and Friends

*Outside ideas of right doing and wrong doing
there is a field. I'll meet you there.*

— Rumi

FAMILY: CAN'T LIVE WITH 'EM, CAN'T LIVE WITHOUT 'EM

I used to have a quote taped up above my bed. It read: "To be great is to be misunderstood." It's one of many of nineteenth-century writer Ralph Waldo Emerson's ingenious statements. I've always loved it because it means that when you are a remarkable person, others won't always get that about you. Haven't you ever noticed that people who are really smart or extra talented don't exactly blend in with the rest of the crowd? Some of the most gifted people have the hardest time fitting in.

Okay, so maybe I'm not a genius, but I can definitely relate to feeling misunderstood. But my older brother used to tease me for thinking I was anything like such a famous, brilliant writer as Emerson. He used to say to me, "Just because you're misunderstood doesn't make you an artist!" The first time I heard these words out of his mouth, I went ballistic on him. I believe my response was "Just because you talk a lot doesn't mean you have anything to say!" and then I proceeded to throw all sorts of things at him. That was before I learned about yoga. The next time he made an obnoxious remark about me, I handled things so much better. I'd been doing yoga for a few weeks by then, and I was much calmer and more comfortable with who I was. Then, when he teased me, my response was simply to take a few deep breaths and walk away. I definitely shocked him big-time by remaining so unaffected and calm! Yoga at work!

I think there is some unwritten, unspoken rule that gives family members the right to tease you without consequence. Your family will always be your family—like it or not. But that doesn't mean you have to react or rebel or even care about the petty little fights and disagreements that go on in your house. Every family is a bit dysfunctional in their own unique way. And I've found the best way to handle it is to remain perfectly calm in the midst of the storm. Rather than throw yourself kicking and screaming into family drama, chances are, you're much more likely to achieve some peace of mind if you can keep it together—at least until you get to your room, where you can stuff your face in a pillow and scream your head off! By not letting your emotions immediately take over, you can also figure out whether you have a battle on your hands that's really worth fighting.

Sometimes, the biggest conflict in the house is that your sister borrowed your brand-new sweater without asking, so you vow never to speak to her again. Other times, it's more serious, like your parents are talking divorce. Or someone very special has just passed away and that has caused emotions to run high for everyone. Part of yoga is to learn to take really dark emotions like anger or anxiety, fear and sadness, and transfer that energy into your yoga practice. Then you will have a clear mind and an open heart when it's time to face your family.

Okay, so now I know you're probably thinking that no one could possibly understand your family dynamics, that you might just as well live in an insane asylum because no one in your house is a remotely rational human being (except for yourself, of course!). Let me tell you something: there is no such thing as a "normal" family. So since you might as well let that fantasy go right now, my suggestion is that you do your best to *accept your family for who they are*. Chances are, they are doing the very best they can as well. And believe it or not, these are the people who will always love you—no matter how loudly you yell!

Take it from Jade, a strong girl and a real firecracker. If yoga can help her deal with the craziness of family, I'm sure it can help you too! According to Jade, after a long day at school, complete with boy drama and annoying teachers:

> *I go home and of course my mom makes everything worse. I was acting really moody and just miserable. That night I went to a yoga class with my stepmom and I really didn't*

wanna go but we had paid in advance so I had to. It was so relaxing and just helped me forget about everything and made me feel so much better about myself. I felt like I was stronger and I acted much more patient toward my mom.

And isn't that what yoga is all about? Feeling stronger, acting calmer, and empowering yourself when you're with the people you love? Of course, your relatives only make up the inner circle of those you love. Then you have your friends.

•••••••• BUDDIES, CHICAS, GIRLIE GIRLS

> Whoever gossips to you, will gossip about you.
> —Spanish Proverb

When you're a teen, your friends may as well be family since you're probably closer to your best friend than you are to your own brother. And it's funny because in my classes, there's never a Lizzie without Eliza, rarely a Molly without Melissa, and Sophia comes to class alone but prefers it when Natalie tags along. Heck, I can hardly stand being away from my best friends! That's girfriends for ya! We need each other. Friends are so valuable because they understand what we are going through, almost as if there was telepathy between us! They have our backs, and we have theirs.

Of course, just as no perfect family exists, neither does a perfect friendship. That's why I have some yogic friendship advice for all you girls out there.

First, girlfriends will come and go, and that's okay. You have to know that some friendships were just not meant to be. Your true friends, however, will always stick around.

Sometimes someone you think is your friend will unexpectedly say something that is really hurtful. Do not take anything personally. Criticisms are always less about you and more about the person making them. Who knows what's really going on with that person? As long as you are the best friend you can be, then that's good enough.

Second, it's important to learn to be a good listener. If you tend to dominate all conversations, that can make other girls feel as if you don't care as much about them as you do about yourself—even if that's totally not the case. Learn to be a good talker too. Check in with yourself and notice if you hold back your feelings, if you are afraid to speak your mind. The rest of us want to know what you're thinking and feeling so we can share in your joy and help you through your sorrow.

Notice if you're being way too influenced by your friends, and then have the courage to break free from what others think and follow your own heart. It's a fine line between your own individuality and being influenced by the group, but as a goddess, I know you have the ability to walk this line with grace and dignity!

Last, when you feel envious or jealous or any other of these very normal but unhealthy feelings toward your girlfriends, just remember this: when you use your energy to wish you had something your friend has or wish the worst for her because you are jealous, you are robbing yourself of the energy you could use to make yourself that much better, that much happier, that much more of a goddess!

Most important, when you are with your friends, have fun!

•••••••••YOGA FOR GETTING ALONG

Breathing with Uddiyana

Uddiyana literally means "in and up." It has an immediate centering effect — crucial when we're dealing with friends and family.

1. Sit in Easy Pose, Butterfly Pose, or on your knees.
2. Inhale deeply.
3. Exhale, and lean your body forward, hands about a foot in front of you on the floor.
4. Once you have exhaled *all the breath out,* pull your belly IN and UP as much as you can.
5. Hold the breath out for a few seconds.
6. Release. Repeat five times.

Chair Pose (Utkatasana)

1. Stand in Mountain Pose.
2. Inhale, and lift your arms above your head, elbows close to your ears.
3. Bend your knees, and lower yourself down as if you were about to sit in a chair.
4. Take three deep breaths, and release the pose.

Twisting Chair Pose
(Parivartana Utkatasana)

1. Stand in Chair Pose, with your hands in prayer position.
2. Inhale, and gently twist from the waist to your right. Bring your left elbow to the outside of your right thigh.
3. Breathe.
4. Repeat on left side.

FYI:
During class, I often ask my students to rest their hands on their navels—their power centers—and just connect with that point. I ask them to go inside of themselves and notice how much of their strength and power they give away to other people in their lives—idolizing other girls, living for a certain boy's attention, taking care of parents or friends before taking care of themselves. Most girls feel that they put very little of their energy into themselves, and that, I explain, often leads to a deep dissatisfaction of self. If you ever feel as if you're giving your power away, just put your hand over your navel. No one will know that you're checking in with your power center. Covering your third chakra with your hand is like plugging up the hole of an energetic leak of your power.

CHAPTER 13

Yoga and Peer Pressure

Keep away from people who try to belittle your ambitions.
Small people always do that, but the really great make you
feel that you, too, can become great.

— Mark Twain

••••• PARTYING, DRUGS, AND ADULT DECISIONS

You know it's a typical day in my yoga class when the girls start off by sitting in a cluster, trading gossip, comparing yoga gear, and laughing in uncontrollable bursts. But today, one girl, Sara, had the rest completely wrapped up in the story she was telling. She was talking about the post-prom party she had gone to the weekend before, and how by 1:00 AM, everyone was completely wasted—except for her.

"Oh my gawd!" screamed one of Sara's yoga buddies, Jen. "How did you deal? I mean, didn't your boyfriend get mad when you didn't drink too?"

"No way. He was totally cool with it. He even told his friends to back off when they teased me for drinking a Coke!"

"That's so sweet!" chimed in another girl. "But didn't you want to at least get a little drunk? I mean, even just a little?"

"Well, um…yeah, kinda. But in my heart, I just felt like it wasn't worth it—you know, getting wasted, dizzy, maybe getting sick, all the things I've seen other friends go through. I was there to have fun, not to lose my mind."

And with that, I knew I had a true yogini on my hands. Sara had actually chosen to remain conscious and aware when all those around her were, as she put it, losing their minds. The fact that Sara stayed sober impressed me, but not nearly as much as her decision to stick to her guns rather than be pressured into something she didn't feel was right for her.

Sometimes you're going to find yourself in situations where the pressures are unavoidable—like Sara did at prom. (I mean, you're not going to miss the social event of the year, right?) And in those situations, resisting peer pressure, whether it's to drink, smoke, or do something you really don't want to do, can be nearly as hard as walking in the sparkly stiletto shoes you had to wear on the special night. It's human nature to feel compelled to do what everyone else around you is doing. So why not choose (when possible) to surround yourself with those who are into being healthy, make you feel good about your decisions, and love you for who you are? Then "being cool" isn't about drinking or getting stoned but about doing whatever feels good for you. I know, I know, you get curious, you want to rebel, you want to try new things, you want to be popular. Every kid in the world feels the same way. So I say, change what the world considers "cool." Be a revolutionary. Get high, but get high off of yoga. You don't have to drop your friends who think "you've gone a little too far with this yoga health-freak thing," but you don't have to follow them either. Your life is your trip, not someone else's, and you get to choose which way to travel on your journey through teendom.

Yoga empowers you to do just that. When the girls are struggling, I always ask them to hold a difficult yoga pose. I tell them, "If you can remain strong in a challenging yoga pose, you can remain strong in challenging life situations." Like Sara, when you find yourself in a position where you're not quite sure which road to take, yoga gives you the confidence to choose the path that feels right for you. You begin to see more clearly that your true friends are those who encourage you to feel your best, not those who convince you to get wasted.

Either define the moment, or the moment will define you.
—Walt Whitman

•••••••It's Not About the Bling

There will always be someone somewhere who has more "stuff" than you have. Some kids are born into outrageous amounts of wealth, some have part-time jobs so they have money to splurge, and some kids have to work so they can chip in to the family pot. No matter where you stand cash-wise, everyone feels the pressure to wear the hottest brand of jeans, sport the most technologically advanced phone/camera/MP3 player, and boast the shiniest bling. Sure, it's fine to have all of that. But it's also fine to have none of it. I don't care what circles you run in or who has what; *what you own does not define who you are.*

So stop where you are, put down the Prada knockoff, step away from your gaggle of girlie pals, and take a few long, deep breaths. Nothing like a little pranayama to ground you, remind you what is real and important, and prevent you from blowing a month's worth of allowance. Possessions are only valuable because we perceive them to be, so start viewing yourself as your most precious, priceless belonging. Then you'll spend only when it's something you sincerely want, not something the rest of the world tells you that you need.

> Without self-esteem, the only change is an exchange
> of masters; with it, there is no need of masters.
> —Gloria Steinem

•••••••• BE A LEADER, NOT A FOLLOWER

As Gloria Steinem points out, if you don't step up to the plate to rule your own life, someone else will. And don't you think it's time to start becoming the master of your own life?

I had an English teacher in tenth grade, Mr. K, who introduced me to two really awesome writers who also wrote about self-reliance: Ralph Waldo Emerson and Henry David Thoreau. Okay, so we didn't officially meet, and they're both dead now, but what these guys had to say was life altering for me. Even though I didn't know it then, these two writers were my introduction to Indian philosophy. It wasn't until I got into yoga that I realized my two favorite writers had been inspired by yoga too! They wrote about the importance of following your own heart. And almost as if they were speaking directly to me, both Emerson and Thoreau encourage you to chart your own course in life. While I'll always wonder if either one of them was hot, because I just know we'd hit it off, it is their philosophy that has never left me. And now I want to pass it on to you.

What you wear and how you look mean nothing in relation to *who you are*. Let the details of your wardrobe, your haircut, and your daily choices reflect the most honest version of yourself you can imagine. Along the road to self-discovery, you will encounter many people — even some whom you love and respect — who will try to persuade you to be just a little less of who you really are. Don't let them.

Sure, it may be a challenge at times; people are always more comfortable around what is familiar to them. But when you shrink back from who you really are, when you remain silent when you have something to say, the whole world becomes a little dimmer. Your individuality—and your expression of it—is what makes all of life interesting and beautiful and bright. Hold back your uniqueness and the world loses a little bit of color, color that becomes the art, music, and magic in our lives. Shine forth who you are and people begin to appreciate you, rather than try to change you. In fact, don't be surprised if others begin to want to be just like you!

WARRIOR POSES

Warrior 1 (Vira Bhadrasana)

When you're standing in Warrior 1 pose, a lot of times you may just feel like giving up. It's a challenging pose that requires all your focus and all your heart. It's a pose that symbolizes where you are in your life right now: on the precipice of something truly great, at the point where you can choose to sink back into complacency and conformity or forge your own path. Be fearless!

1. Stand in Mountain Pose.
2. Step your left foot forward about three feet. Keep your knee bent at 90 degrees, ideally.
3. Step your right leg back and turn your right foot out slightly.

4. Square your hips to the front of your body.
5. Inhale, and lift your arms up above your head.
6. Exhale, and sink lower into the pose.
7. Breathe here for three to five breaths.
   Repeat with your right leg forward.

Warrior 2 (Vira Bhadrasana)

1. Stand in Warrior 1 pose (left foot forward).
2. Inhale, and rotate your hips to the right so your body is now fully open to the right side.
3. Bring your arms down and out to the sides of your body so that they are parallel with the floor.
4. Breathe here for three to five breaths. Repeat on the other side.

MANTRAS:

* ❃ I decide what's right for myself.
* ❃ I trust in the decisions that are right for me.
* ❃ My path is up to me, not my friends or peers.
* ❃ I can walk away and still be loved.

CHAPTER 14

Yoga and School

We cannot teach people anything; we can only
help them discover it within themselves.

— Galileo Galilei

•••••• FOCUS TO START THE DAY

Coffee is super yum and it definitely gets the blood pumping and the hands shaking (or maybe that's just me on too much caffeine), but doing some yoga when you wake up will give you energy without giving you the shakes. I know: you stayed up too late on the phone talking to your best friend because neither of you could believe what just happened on that night's episode of the new WB show. The last thing you want to do is get out of bed and go to school! A few long, deep breaths and some morning stretches will help you wake up, even on those cold, dark mornings when you'd rather eat live bugs than leave your bed. Yoga will also clear your head when all the day's questions begin to flood your brain before you've even had your cereal: What should I wear today? Did I study enough for the algebra test? Will there be a world war today? I know, you are exhausted and you'd much rather just hide from the world than face scary Mr. Brewster in history class. Of course, it would be nice to run into the hot foreign-exchange student. Plus, you really have no choice, according to your dad. Thank goodness for yoga that awakens and energizes!

·········TESTS, STRESS, AND ACADEMIC SUCCESS

For weeks, one of my students was working on a term paper. She had to write an analytical essay discussing the symbolism in Charlotte Brontë's novel *Jane Eyre*. I know she put her heart and soul into that paper, which was going to be worth 50 percent of her class grade for the term. Turns out, she got a B+. That bothered her, but not as much as the girl in her class who bragged that she got an A and had only worked on the paper for a week. Ugh!

In my experience, grades are one of the biggest causes of stress. To me, a bad grade was equivalent to being called a big dummy. But girls, this is not true. Even though it is very important to work hard and do well in school so we can get into good colleges and do something meaningful and productive with our lives, grades do not determine our worth as people. (As if we could be defined by a letter!) They are simply a way for teachers to assess how we are doing academically. I had a teacher in high school who used to say, "My students are people!

I hate grading them as if they were meat! But according to the system, I have no choice." Aiming for good grades is just something you *have* to do as a student. And it is possible to do it without losing your mind. So how do you handle the stress of looming paper deadlines? Of final exams? Or of the biggies like the SAT?

First, you breathe. Long, deep inhales and exhales. Then, when you need something more, you can practice yoga exercises specifically meant to calm your mind and body (described at the end of this chapter). Then you do your very best on whatever assignment you have to do. Encourage yourself. Sip hot tea while you work. Suck on sour apple hard candies. But do not slam yourself with negative comments, because that's definitely not going to help you get better grades.

Occasionally, even when you work your hardest, you're going to get a lower grade than you had expected. In fact, many times, it seems that the more committed we are to our goal, the more the universe wants to keep us from achieving it. But that's how you know you are moving forward in your life. Think about it: if you were standing still, not going anywhere, you wouldn't feel any opposition. Only when you're moving forward do you encounter the wind in your face. And the opposition you experience is really just the universe testing you. It's like the superpower in the sky is saying to you, "Oh, so you want something? How badly do you really want it? You have to show me!" I don't know about you, but when I really want something in my life—I mean really, truly, wholeheartedly want something—nothing gets in my way.

So then how do you ace academia when, even at your best, you feel like you're not getting anywhere? You maintain a vision of your goals. You take all of your intentions for school (or whatever it is you are trying to attain or achieve) and hold them in a sacred space in your heart and mind. You do your yoga and trust in its ability to work. Then you tell the universe to bring it—just like Eliza did when finals were quickly approaching:

> *A few weeks ago, I had finals. I'd been studying nonstop for two weeks, and the only breaks I took were meals and sometimes swimming for a half hour. I was getting very overwhelmed with all the information, and I was getting bad headaches, and it was hard for me to sleep.... Even though I really didn't have time to spare, I went to yoga. It totally took my mind off of finals.*
>
> *When the class was over, I was so relaxed. I felt like I had the strength to run a few miles, and I had forgotten about my final exams.... Yoga helped me stay calm during my finals too. I would just think about staying calm and not rushing and staying true to my instincts about my answers.*

Eliza was totally overwhelmed and yoga helped make all the difference. Sophia had a similar experience with school-related stress. As she said, "I used to get really nervous when I had a large homework load....Now my response is more like, 'I can handle it.'"

And so can you. Here are some exercises to help you focus, relax, and concentrate when it comes to school.

······ YOGA @ HOME

To help you focus when you're studying, writing papers, and preparing for class.

Seated Forward Bend (Paschimottanasana)
(see chapter 8)

Tree Pose (Vrksasana)

This pose will help you to reestablish your focus and mental balance when you become overwhelmed with your studies or that annoying paper on The Odyssey that you are writing.

1. Stand up.
2. Bring your right leg up and rest the bottom of your right foot on the inside of your left thigh.

3. After you have found your balance, slowly raise your hands to prayer position.
4. Breathe long and deep, focusing your eyes on a spot in front of you.

Downward-Facing Dog (You know this one!)
(see chapter 5)

• • • • • • • YOGA @ SCHOOL

To practice while you are at school sitting at your desk, at your locker, or just wherever, so that you can calm a restless mind and focus on the task at hand.

Alternate Nostril Breathing
(see chapter 3)

Heart Over Head

Simply let your head fall toward your feet while sitting at your desk. (Pretend you dropped something on the floor and then hang there for a few.) Doing this allows the blood to flow to your brain, reverses gravity

on your body, and brings a sense of renewal and clarity to your mind so that you can get back to work.

•••••• MANTRAS:

- ❊ I trust my instincts and my decisions to be the right choices.
- ❊ All of the answers reside within me.
- ❊ I prevail through the hardest of challenges.
- ❊ I can achieve anything I strive to achieve.

> **FYI:**
> Saraswati is the Indian goddess of wisdom, knowledge, music, and art. Even if you don't believe in the mythology of yoga, it couldn't hurt to give Saraswati a little shout-out whenever you could use a hand in the brain department!

Teachers open the door, but you must enter by yourself.
—Chinese Proverb

Chapter 15

Yoga and Sleeping

> I sleep. A lot. I do yoga and go to museums.... I decided
> when my dad died, I'm going to do more of that and not
> work myself to death for no reason.
> — Gwyneth Paltrow

STAYING UP ALL NIGHT, SLEEPING ALL DAY

"I swear, if I don't get a good night's sleep tonight, I'm going to bite someone's head off! And I'm a vegetarian!" That's how Ali introduced herself to me and to the rest of the girls at her first yoga class. Ali had problems sleeping at night, and as we all know, sleep deprivation is not a good thing when trying to learn about Hemingway during third period. Frustrated that her daughter spent the midnight hours in front of a buzzing TV rather than sleeping soundly, Ali's mom suggested she join some of her friends at yoga. What Ali needed most was to retrain her nervous system to mellow out at night so she could eventually fall asleep. According to Ali, "As soon as it got dark, that's when I would get all my energy. Then forget about it. I'm up all night."

A tiny dancer, Ali was clearly a powerhouse of strength and determination. But her tendency to overachieve was getting in the way of her much-needed resting time—mostly because she had so much going on in her life and in her mind, she was overloaded. In other words, a stress case.

Stress is the number one obstacle to sleep. Even the slightest change in our lives can cause enough stress to turn our nights into days and days into nights. Our lifestyle also plays a major role in affecting many teens' favorite pastime: sleeping. As it turned out, Ali was drinking coffee after dinner, had to babysit her little brother while doing her homework at night, diligently did her chores around the house, and was also extremely dedicated to her ballet practice. So really, she didn't have much going on in her life. Yeah, right! The kind of responsibility Ali had was the kind usually reserved for adults, not teenage girls! Unfortunately, teens have to take on more and more these days, which makes their sleep time all the more vital. Clearly, Ali's sleep problems came from a crazy amount of stress.

But you don't have to be juggling knives to feel a little stressed out. Sometimes we just feel overwhelmed with everything going on in our lives or weighed down by the seriousness of the world today. Everyone gets stressed out at one point or another. And we could all benefit from a good night's sleep. But first we have to learn to take our stress levels down—or else we'll be up all night counting sheep and watching *Late Night with Conan O'Brien*.

·······I'M NOT LAZY, I'M TIRED!

Sleep deprivation is a real thing among teens! It's a biological fact, and I'm here to help back you girls up on this fact. You naturally stay up longer and need to sleep more hours. And I'm not just talking "beauty rest" here, I'm talking about a whole shift in the natural sleep cycle of teens. No wonder you've often thought that getting your teeth pulled out, one by one, without any novocaine, would be less painful than first period.

I believe I can make things happen, but I'm certainly not capable of single-handedly changing the entire country's school system. (You'll be happy to hear that some schools are actually starting class an hour later because of sleepy students!) Instead, I want to give you gals some helpful exercises that can help you get to sleep when an early wake-up call is looming, and some to help you keep your eyes open when they feel like bricks weighing down your face midway through algebra. Ashley's yoga has helped her to get to sleep, but Jessie uses her yoga to stay awake:

> *Just today I was feeling so tired because I stayed up really late doing homework. I came to school totally out of it. Then I did yoga, and all the breathing and stretches really woke me up and because of it I was able to stay awake during my next class.*

Getting adequate sleep doesn't just help you do well intellectually, it helps you feel better emotionally. Ever notice how down and out you feel when you didn't sleep well the night before? You'll be a much happier girl if you can get through the school day with your eyes open and feeling energized—even if you did learn how to cook a chocolate soufflé on the Food Network at 3:00 AM.

•••••••••"WAKE ME UP!" YOGA

Stretch Pose (with Kapala-bhati breathing)

1. Lie flat on your back.
2. Inhale, and lift your head and legs three to six inches off the bed.
3. Practice a few rounds of Kapala-bhati breathing (see chapter 3).

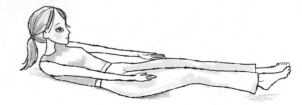

Cat Stretch

1. Lying on your back, bend your left knee and cross it over the right side of your body.

2. Reach your left arm out to the left, and place your right hand on your right knee to help you in the stretch.

3. Stay here for five to ten long, deep breaths.

4. Repeat with your right leg crossing over the left side.

"LET ME SLEEP!" YOGA

Shoulder Stand (Sarvangasana)

Shoulder stand is a good one to do just before you climb into bed. It calms your nervous system and stimulates glands (thyroid and parathyroid) that help your body chill out. It's especially great to practice if you have trouble sleeping on a regular basis. Do Bridge Pose (see chapter 4) first to prepare yourself for this pose.

1. Lie on your back with your knees bent in toward your chest. Find a comfy position for your neck, then leave it there.

2. Inhale, and lift your hips off the ground.

3. Bend your arms and place your hands on your lower back to

support you from lowering back down.

4. Slowly straighten your legs as you lift your hips higher, and slide your hands along your back to support yourself.

5. Breathe deeply here for as long as feels comfortable. Check in with your body to make sure you are not in any pain and that your weight is on your shoulders and upper back—not your neck.

6. To come down, slowly lower yourself, placing your weight onto your hands.

Left Nostril Breathing
(see chapter 3)

The left nostril is associated with the right side of the brain. Just breathing through this side produces a calming effect on the entire nervous system.

Rub the Soles of the Feet Together

This is one I learned from Guru Singh. There are something like 72,000 nerve endings in our hands and feet, and this is like a soothing massage for them. You wouldn't think it, but just rubbing the bottoms of your feet together can help you find your way to never-never land.

Instead of getting all tweaked out and frustrated if you can't sleep at night, the best yoga exercise is to practice just being in the present moment. Breathing deeply, enjoying the coziness and warmth of your bed, and listening to all of the night's sounds can help you relax. I've always found that lying in bed at night is one of the best times to learn to accept things exactly as they are in the here and now.

MANTRAS, OR BEDTIME WISDOM:

- ❁ I have nowhere to be and nothing to do.
- ❁ All I have to do is breathe and relax.
- ❁ I am at peace with my life.
- ❁ I give up all my worries and problems to the universe to take care of while I sleep.
- ❁ I am warm and cozy and ready to dream.

CHAPTER 16

Overcoming Obstacles

(And How Not to Be Afraid of the Dark)

The greater the obstacle, the more glory
in overcoming it.

— Moliere

My yoga teacher, Guru Singh, always tells his students that in order to reach the light, we must first move through the darkness. To me, going through change is like going through the darkness: it's scary and sometimes even painful, but I know that if I keep on walking forward, I will eventually reach the light. Normally, we tend to shy away from change. I mean, who wants to experience any kind of distress or discomfort when we could just turn around and get back in bed? It is our human nature to avoid the places that scare us. But these are the very places we must go in order to get to where we want to be. I know, seems about as fair as when the captain of the cheerleading squad gets voted homecoming queen. But we cannot quit simply because we are afraid to try or because we are convinced that we are incapable of succeeding. I know this to be true not just because great yoga teachers, loving parents, and respected mentors have said it to me, but from my own experience.

It has been my goal to teach yoga since the very first day that I became a student. Then, just as I began to teach, I was injured and tore all the tendons and ligaments in my right shoulder. Not only would I have to put my dreams of teaching aside, but I was also forced to stop my yoga practice as I'd known it and endure three shoulder surgeries and many months of physical therapy. Worst of all, the doctors believed I'd never be strong enough to stand on my hands again—and that meant no Downward-Facing Dog either.

How was I going to be a yoga teacher if I couldn't even practice? I froze. I didn't know how to surpass this huge barrier that now stood between me and my life plans. For many months, I believed that my whole future as a teacher was over. I let this self-defeating belief guide me until I realized that if I wanted to get back to yoga, I would have to change my attitude. It was going to take courage and resolve to overcome my shoulder injury and teach again. I had to believe that anything was possible.

The moment I took on this mind-set, the moment I chose to become a warrior and a true yogini, all sorts of incredible things began to occur. I noticed how much stronger my shoulder had become from all of the physical therapy I'd been doing. I grew increasingly confident that I was going to teach again. I knew I was going back to my yoga warriors very soon. I took on the mind-set of a guru—one who gladly enters the darkness because she knows the light awaits her. It's knowing that in order to get an A, you must bear the burden of studying; in order to get the part in the play, you must take a risk and audition.

In order to conquer the challenges and changes in our lives, we must let go of our fears and our false conceptions of who we are. We must risk failing, falling, not knowing quite where we are going, but all the while having the faith that we will end up okay. Renee was afraid she'd look like a clown in yoga, and now she's a star in class. Rachel was scared to live a day of her life without being stoned, and now her mind and body are so clear, she is accomplishing goals she never dreamed possible. Doing yoga enables us to tap into this inner strength and confidence. (Just think of doing yoga like trying out for the dance team or studying for a big exam—it may take some work until you achieve your goal, but once you do, you feel as though you can accomplish anything!)

Once we accept our limits, we go beyond them.
—Albert Einstein

Triangle Pose
(Trikonasana)

This pose stretches the hips, enabling you to feel more open and grounded to the earth. And when you feel more stable, you are more likely to take risks. It is also a chest opener that frees up your heart to all that the world has to offer to you.

1. Stand with your feet about three feet apart.
2. Turn your right foot out 90 degrees so your toes are straight out to the right and the left foot is slightly turned in.
3. Inhale, and lift both your arms out to the side and extend your body toward your left side.
4. Exhale, and fold to the side, bringing your right hand down to your right leg and your left arm up to the ceiling.
5. Breathe three deep breaths.
6. Inhale, and come back to standing.
7. Switch sides.

Half Moon Pose
(Ardhal Chandrasana)

This pose comes pretty darn close to allowing you to feel entirely free, since your body is opening up in all directions. It requires balance (you can also practice against a wall) and patience, but it will only strengthen your resolve to soar higher in your life.

1. Come into Triangle Pose (on the right side).
2. Place your right hand on the floor and shift all your weight onto your right foot.
3. Inhale, and reach your left leg straight out behind you and your left arm up toward the ceiling.
4. Exhale, and find your balance.
5. Breathe long and deep, reaching out through the left leg and up through the left hand.
6. Slowly come back down into Triangle Pose.
7. Switch sides.

MEDITATION FOR GANESHA, "REMOVER OF OBSTACLES"

Ganesha is a Hindu deity who is represented by a creature with an elephant head and a big belly. He is the creator and remover of obstacles. You do not have to really believe in Ganesha as a god to benefit from what he represents. The following is a mantra you can chant to ask the universe for protection, prosperity, and peace.

OM Ganesha Namah
OM, Shanti, Shanti, Shanti

Chant, sing, or recite this mantra until you feel a sense of peace come over you.

CHAPTER 17

The Girl Goddess in All of Us

God is seated in the hearts of all.
— Bhagavad Gita (c. BC 400)

I don't think most girls know how absolutely incredible they are — how beautiful, inspiring, and powerful every single one of us really is. That's mostly because we have been raised in a culture that tells us that only if we are skinny, have a hot boy by our side, and make the big bucks are we okay. But the truth is, every girl is a miraculous product of God, the universe, Buddha, Allah — whatever you want to call that which gives us the gift of life. We are awesome, simply because we were born. Yoga teaches us to thrive off of this concept and off of the happy energy that comes with this way of thinking. Yoga also teaches that each one of us was put on this planet for a purpose. (Yes, even the kid who threatened to cut off your braids in math class is here for a reason!)

A Shout-Out to the Universe (or, Being Grateful)

I recently met a cute guy at a party who told me that he believes he has lived a perfect storybook life. I responded as any girl with a secret crush would: "Dude, you are so full of yourself!"

But on my drive home, I thought about what he had said and realized that perhaps this guy wasn't necessarily being stuck-up. Maybe, just maybe, he was simply expressing his gratitude for the wonderful life he had lived. Most of us spend so much of our energy lamenting all of the bad things in our lives, all of our problems and faults and shortcomings, that we end up in a pretty miserable state of mind. We've become so used to being whiners that we find it unbelievable (and kinda nauseating) when we meet someone who is actually content with his or her life! But any yogi will tell you that gratitude is one of the most powerful practices you can use to change your life for the better.

You can think of yoga as your gratitude guide. It lifts your mood and clears your mind so that you can start to see beauty where before you only saw blah. Your heart opens, and you naturally begin to feel how lucky you are in this life. Life is hectic, I know, so you're never going to be in appreciation mode 24/7. But yoga can help you get there at least some of those hours. Even practiced yogis view gratitude as a waking meditation, something we must consciously remind ourselves to do. When you finally stop and take a minute to give thanks for all of the wonderful things in your life, the little things that once bothered you don't seem like such a big deal anymore. Over time, you'll begin to realize for yourself that happiness doesn't come from getting what you want, but from wanting what you've already got—and then simply saying "thank you."

You, My Girl, Are a Pocket Devi

A "pocket devi" is a mini goddess! She is a girl who embodies all of the qualities—mental, emotional, and physical—of a divine female being. And that is exactly who you are. If you don't know it already, it's time to truly know how sexy, beautiful, and fabulous you really are.

It is actually our duty to praise ourselves, to honor our spirits and our bodies, and to let our inner light shine brightly. If we shrink back from the world, if we slouch our shoulders because we are ashamed of our bodies, if we hold ourselves back just to make others comfortable, we are not living to our fullest potential. If you choose to live in the dark, and hide away from the challenges of the world, you will never know how wonderful the warm sun feels on your face, how fulfilling it is to help someone in need, how rewarding it is to shine your light where only darkness exists. You need to believe that your presence in the world actually benefits the world. I don't care who you are, what you look like, where you are from, what kind of family you come from, or how much money you have. You must believe that you have the ability to achieve even your wildest dreams because, well, why the heck not? After all, god (or whatever higher spirit you believe in) exists in some form within us all, so you have to figure, if god can make so much happen in this world, so can you.

I know that sometimes it is hard to believe that you have the power to create your own reality, but take it from someone who knows what it's like to be a teenage girl in these crazy times. Yoga taught me how to walk forward even when I wanted to run back home. Now it's your turn.

········YOGA FOR FINAL RELAXATION

Knees to Chest

1. Lie on your back.
2. Bring both knees up to your chest, and wrap your arms around your legs.
3. Breathe several long, deep breaths.

Corpse Pose (Savasana)

This is by far everyone's favorite pose. It always comes at the very end of the class and is meant to allow all of the energy you have awakened during your yoga practice to flow throughout your body. It is also deeply relaxing. Practice this at the end of a full sequence of poses, or just when you need a break from the world. I like to put on some new age-y, Enya-type music for this pose.

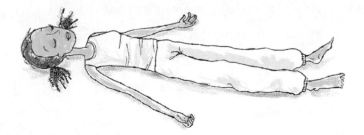

1. Lie on your back, with your hands on the floor and palms facing up.
2. Close your eyes.
3. From the tips of your toes to the top of your head, fully relax.
4. Let your body sink into the ground below you, allowing the breath to flow in and out naturally.
5. Let go of every part of your body. Deeply relax.

········THE MEDITATION TO HONOR YOURSELF

I call this one the "I rock" meditation. Not really an ancient Indian mantra, but one that I find works just the same.

- ❧ Grab a piece of notebook paper—yeah, go ahead, just rip it out of your English binder.
- ❧ Now make a list of five things you are grateful for in your life. Below that, make a list of five things you would like to achieve or accomplish in the coming days, months, or years.
- ❧ Place that paper on the floor in front of you.
- ❧ Turn on a great song, anything that has a really good vibe.
- ❧ Sit in Easy Pose, spine long and straight, shoulders down and back. Place your hands on your knees, palms facing up.
- ❧ Now close your eyes and get into the song. Sing loudly and freely, and pay no attention to the sound of your singing voice—I promise you, it's beautiful.
- ❧ Now this may seem totally corny, but I actually like to sing what I've written on my paper to the tune of the song.
- ❧ Practice for seven to ten minutes.

Now tell me you don't feel like you could fly.

THE GLOSSARY

Abhaya: Fearlessness.

Anahata: "Unstuck," in Sanskrit. Refers to the fourth chakra, the heart center, when it is fully opened through yoga.

Asana: Posture or position in yoga. Means "to be present."

Aura: The electromagnetic field of energy that surrounds every individual. Doing yoga strengthens our mental, physical, and spiritual bodies, which helps to give us a strong and radiant aura.

Basic Abs: Small, isolated stomach crunches that strengthen the body's core muscles.

Bhagavad Gita: The most famous "song" or epic work of Hindu philosophy, spiritual wisdom, and yoga.

Bhakti: A devotional form of yoga. For example, when you help out a friend with homework or volunteer to pick up your little brother from soccer practice, you are doing a good deed, or Bhakti yoga.

Breath of Fire (Kapala-bhati): Rapid inhalation and exhalation through the nose to achieve a heightened state of awareness. Also acts as a cleansing and detoxifying form of pranayama.

Bridge Pose (Setu Bandha Sarvangasana): Heart opener and beginning back bend, done by lying flat on your back and lifting your lower torso, bottom tucked under, several inches off the floor. See p. 41.

Buddha: An enlightened one.

Butterfly Pose (Baddha Konasana): Seated position in which the soles of the feet are pressed together, allowing your knees to fall to either side of the body. See p. 40.

Camel Pose (Ustrasana): Heart opener and more challenging back bend. Performed by sitting on your knees and gently leaning back until you can grab the soles of your feet. See p. 60.

Chair Pose (Utkatasana): Powerful standing pose to strengthen legs and increase endurance. Twisting Chair Pose is a more challenging version of the same pose. See p. 123.

Chakra: An energy center. Each of the seven chakras is associated with a nerve center in the body.

Chandra: The moon.

Child's Pose (Balasana): Resting pose. Sit on your heels and bring your head to the floor, arms by your side. See p. 61.

Cobra Pose (Bhujanga-asana): Easy back bend performed by lying on your belly, elbows placed below your shoulders, so your forearms press onto the floor. Push up and arch your back slightly. Integral position in Sun Salutations. See p. 68.

Cooper: Last name of a dedicated and devoted yoga teacher and writer (me!).

Corpse Pose (Savasana): Resting pose done at the end of every yoga practice. It is the time during which your entire body is recharged as a result of the yoga (and generally everyone's favorite part of yoga!). See p. 159.

Cow/Cat Pose: Combination of two poses, both done on hands and knees, that warm up the body by arching and flexing the spine. See p. 50.

Crisscross Abs: Core strengthening abdominal crunches. In coordination with the breath, lift your right elbow to your left knee, come back to center, then bring your left elbow to your right knee. See p. 89.

Devi: A goddess.

Downward-Facing Dog (Adho Mukha Savasana): Most commonly practiced inversion. Stretches shoulders, arms, and entire back of the body. Acts as a mood lifter. See p. 51.

Drishti: Your gaze, or what you are looking at while meditating.

Ganesha: The Hindu elephant god who symbolizes prosperity and protection.

Guru: In its literal translation, "guru" means that which takes us from darkness (gu) into light (ru). The Sanskrit word "guru" also means "weighty," which refers to someone of great importance.

Gyan Mudra: The most common hand position used in meditations. The index finger and thumb meet, while the other three fingers are held straight out.

Half Moon Pose (Ardhal Chandrasana): Balancing and opening pose. Elicits a sense of openness and freedom, as the entire body stretches out in all directions. See p. 153.

Happy Baby Pose: Restorative pose done by lying flat on your back with your legs pulled down toward your chest, hands grasping the soles of your feet. See p. 96.

Hatha: Its philosophic meaning is the union between the sun and the moon. Most commonly used to describe a widely practiced form of physical yoga. Other styles of yoga include Iyengar, Ashtanga, Bikram, Viniyoga, Kripalu, Integral, Anusara, Ananda, Kundalini, Somatic, Jivamukti, etc.

Heartsong: The poetry your heart writes. Term coined by Mattie Stepanek (peacemaker and poet, 1990-2004).

Hero Pose (Virasana): Seated, restorative pose with knees bent, and feet spread to either side of your bottom. Balances the second chakra, center of creativity and productivity. See p. 59.

Horse Stance: Standing pose with your feet spread wide apart, legs bent so that your thighs are parallel to the floor. Works on the first chakra to help you feel grounded and committed to your intentions. See p. 48.

Inversions: Any pose in which the heart is raised above the head so that the effect of gravity is reversed on the body and blood can circulate to the brain. Inversions help to lift depression.

Kapala-bhati (Breath of Fire): Rapid inhalation and exhalation through the nose to achieve a heightened state of awareness. Also acts as a cleansing and detoxifying form of pranayama.

Karma: The cosmic law of cause and effect. In other words, if you cheat on a test, in some form or another, it's gonna come back and kick you in the butt.

Kundalini: The creative potential of every person. Kundalini exists as energy within our body. Also refers to a specific practice of yoga, known as Kundalini yoga.

Lion's Breath: Pranayama (breathing) where you take the greatest inhale, stick your tongue out, and roar like a lion, releasing all tension and negativity from your body. Best practiced in Horse Stance or lunge position.

Lotus Pose (Padma asana): Favorite meditation posture for yogis. This is the classic seated asana in which each foot rests on the opposing thigh. Viewed by yogis as a remedy to all ailments.

Mantra: Mind's projection of prayer. Can be a thought, word, or phrase expressed in sound.

Mountain Pose (Tadasana): Basis for all standing poses, practiced by standing tall, feet hip-width apart, shoulders rolled back and down, seat tucked under. Improves posture and poise. See p. 98.

Mudra: Asanas—or poses—for the hands that each have a different effect on the body. Two common mudras are the anjali mudra (hands pressed together in prayer position) and gyan mudra (thumbs and forefingers pressing together).

Nadi-shodhana: Alternate nostril breathing. Purifies and calms the body.

OM: The sound of the universe in perfect harmony. Recited as a mantra to get in tune with the universal flow of all life.

"Ong Namo Guru Dev Namo": A mantra that translates as "I honor the teacher within my own being." This is the mantra always used to "tune in" before a Kundalini yoga class is taught.

Patanjali: Author of the most famous yoga teachings, *The Yoga Sutras*, thousands of years ago.

Prana: Life energy that we take in through the breath.

Pranayana: The practice of breath control, central to any yoga practice.

Prayer position (Anjali Mudra): Hands pressed together at the center of the chest.

Prayer Squats (Malasana): Exercise to strengthen the first chakra, the root chakra. Place hands in prayer position, and position feet slightly more than hip-width apart. Bend knees in a squat. See p. 113.

Ray of Light Twist: Performed by sitting on the floor, right leg outstretched before you, left leg bent with your foot placed near the inner thigh of your right leg. Sit up straight and reach your right arm against the outside of your left knee and twist.

All twists aid digestion and free tension in your spine and back. See p. 88.

Sadhana: A spiritual discipline, or what you would call your daily yoga practice.

Saraswati: "She Who Flows." Goddess of the arts and education.

Sat: Infinite Truth.

Sat Naam: A mantra that means "Truth is my identity."

Savasana: "Corpse Pose," or final resting pose done at the end of any yoga practice. See p. 159.

Scorpion Variation Pose (Caravakasana): Beginning form of a very advanced pose. Strengthens shoulders, opens hips, and increases overall flexibility. See p. 103.

Seated Forward Bend (Paschimottanasana): With your legs outstretched before you, place your hands on your knees, shins, or ankles. Inhale, and reach forward with a flat back on the exhale. Improves mood and increases energy. See p. 76.

Seated Straddle Pose (Upavistha Konasana): Similar to Seated Forward Bend, but your legs are stretched out to either side so that they form a V. Balances second chakra, your center of creativity and sexuality. See p. 114.

Serotonin: Chemical in the brain that elicits feelings of contentment and peace of mind. Yoga has been proven to increase the amount of serotonin that is released in the brain. In other words, it helps get rid of the blues so you can feel extraordinary!

Shakti: The feminine power of creation; woman.

Shanti: Peace.

Shiva: The masculine power of stability. Shiva and Shakti together represent a perfect balance of life, just like the sun and the moon.

Shoulder Stand (Sarvangasana): Soothing pose practiced toward the end of a yoga set. Stimulates circulation, enhances digestion, and mellows out any kinks in the nervous system. An inversion practiced by placing the body's weight on your back and shoulders, while your legs extend straight up into the air. See p. 145.

Sitali Pranayam: "Cooling" or calming breath, practiced by inhaling through a curled tongue and exhaling through the nostrils.

Standing Forward Bend (Uttanasana): Feet hip-width apart, your torso bends at the waist so the body hangs forward. Practiced as a warm-up for other standing poses or on its own to release tension in the back, neck, and hamstrings. See p. 98.

Straddle Abs: Basic abs practiced with legs lifted off the ground and extended out to the sides in a V. Incredibly useful for getting in touch with the lower belly and organs reserved for us girlies! See p. 102.

Stretch Pose: Third chakra or power center strengthener. Lie flat on your back. Lift your head, chest, legs, and feet three to six inches off the ground for thirty seconds. Release. See p. 144.

Sun Salutations (Surya Namaskara): Series of postures in Hatha yoga that are performed as a devotional practice to the sun, without which there would be no life. See p. 66.

Surya: The sun.

Third Eye: The sixth chakra, associated with intuition and wisdom.

Tree Pose (Vrksasana): Standing asana performed by placing the sole of one foot on the inner thigh of the opposite leg, hands placed in prayer position at the center of the chest. Tree Pose increases focus, concentration, and balance. See p. 137.

Triangle Pose (Trikonasana): Standing pose that opens the chest and stretches the hips and legs. See p. 152.

Uddiyana: Form of pranayama that literally means "in and up." After a complete exhalation, the belly is pulled in and up toward the chest. This is an advanced practice that increases a yogi's awareness. See p. 122.

Ujjayi: Form of pranayama practiced consistently throughout one's yoga practice. As the yogini breathes deeply through her nose, she allows the throat to constrict slightly so it sounds as if she is doing her best Darth Vader impression. Increases energy and cleanses the entire body.

Ultimate Core Balance (Navasana): Seated asana that strengthens the third chakra. Lift legs about 60 degrees off the floor, and extend arms directly in front of you. A challenging pose that increases balance and core strength. See p. 79.

Upanishads: The sacred philosophical texts of Hindu literature.

Warrior Poses (Vira Bhadrasana): Standing poses that strengthen your legs, root you to the earth, and inspire your inner goddess to bravely shine forth. See p. 130.

Yogi/Yogini: One who does yoga.

Mantras, Music, and Good Stuff to Read

To tune in to your inner self before you practice yoga or before you need to focus or concentrate:

Ong Namo Guru Dev Namo

(I honor the teacher within my own being.)

When you are fearful, stressed out, or waiting for the boy you like to call you back:

Om Namah Shivaya

(I honor the teacher within myself.)

When you find out that your boyfriend told your best friend that he was going to break up with you for the new foreign-exchange student:

Time for a new and better boyfriend.

(a perfectly acceptable mantra)

When you first wake up in the morning and dread going to school:

I am beautiful.

I am ready to take on the day.

For when you need energy and good luck:

Har Harray Haree, Wah Hey Guru

(Prosperity and peace are with me.)

When you need to be reminded that everything and anything is possible, that you have the power to create your own reality:

Hummee Hum Brum Hum

(What I am to be, I already am!)

When you need some peace of mind and clarity:

Om, Om, Om…

Simply sit, focus on the breath, and meditate on "OM" or the mantra of your choice.

······ Yoga Sequence for Your Own At-Home Class

After you chant some mantras, try the following sequence at home:

Breathing (chapter 3)

Forward bends (chapters 4, 8)

Abs (chapters 8, 9)

Bridge Pose (chapter 4)

Sun Salutations (chapter 7)

Warrior Poses (chapter 13)

Relaxation poses — Knees to Chest (chapter 17)

Savasana (chapter 17)

Meditation of your choice

Music to Inspire and Empower

Bob Marley (reggae: uplifting)

U2 (incomparable rock: motivating and meaningful)

India.Arie (soul pop: inspiring)

Ani DiFranco (moody alternative rock: girl power!)

Lauryn Hill, *The Miseducation of Lauryn Hill* (soul, rap, and empowering lyrics)

Seal (R&B sung by a yogi: spiritual, beautiful, harmonic)

Destiny's Child and Beyoncé (R&B: girl power)

Avril Lavigne (girl goddess punk rock and melodic tunes)

Aretha Franklin (queen of soul: R&B)

Alicia Keys (successor to Aretha! Jazzy, soul tunes)

Music You Can Groove to

John Mayer (guitar-driven, grooving pop rock)

Nelly Furtado (jazz filled pop: upbeat, motivating)

Maroon 5 (pop-rock doesn't get happier than this)

Outkast, *Speakerboxx* (rap, rock, pop, soul. Eclectic, incredible, dynamic)

Gavin DeGraw (piano-driven, pop)

Justin Timberlake (fun, melodic tunes you can dance to)

Joss Stone (powerhouse of soul: Brit who sings her butt off)

Favorite Anytime Tunes

Ben Harper (soulful rock & ballads)
Coldplay (only the best rock band of the 21st century: moody, meaningful Brit pop)
Counting Crows (beautiful moody rock)
Joni Mitchell (bluesy, folk rock)
The Black Crowes (best blues rock around)
Bob Dylan (masterful poetics and innovator of folk rock)
Ryan Adams (California folk rock: melodic, moody)
Sheryl Crowe (good ole grooving rock and roll)
Michelle Branch (powerful pop-rock)
Lenny Kravitz, *Believe* (smooth, insightful soul rock)
The Indigo Girls (beautiful, harmonic folk rock)
Alanis Morrissette (alternative, empowering, rock)
Cat Stevens (70s acoustic folk rock: inspiring)
Jason Mraz (reggae, rock, and pop: upbeat, fun tunes, with fantastic lyrics)
Sarah McLachlan (angelic, intense rock)
Frou Frou (ethereal, electronic rock)

Music for Yoga and Meditation

Krishna Das
Deva Premal
Deepak Chopra

Jai Uttal

Angelique Kidjo

Guru Singh & Co.

Enya

Enigma

Deep Forest

Wah

Bhagavan Das

BOOKS & POETRY

The Alchemist by Paulo Coelho

The Bhagavad Gita by Barbara Miller

The Beauty Myth by Naomi Wolf

The Celestine Prophecy by James Redfield

Don't Sweat the Small Stuff by Richard Carlson

e. e. cummings's poetry

The Essential Rumi by Coleman Barks

The Giving Tree by Shel Silverstein

Harry Potter and the Sorcerer's Stone by J. K. Rowling

Heartsongs by Mattie Stepanek

Henry David Thoreau's essays, "Civil Disobedience" and "Walden"

I Know Why the Caged Bird Sings by Maya Angelou

Jane Eyre by Charlotte Brontë

Letters to a Young Poet by Rainer Maria Rilke

Little Women by Louisa May Alcott

Oh, the Places You'll Go by Dr. Seuss

The Places That Scare You by Pema Chödrön

Ralph Waldo Emerson's essays, "Self-Reliance" and "Nature"

Revolution from Within by Gloria Steinem

Shambhala: The Sacred Path of the Warrior by Chogyam Trungpa

Siddhartha by Herman Hesse

Succulent Wild Women by Sark

Walt Whitman, *Leaves of Grass* and *Song of Myself*

The Yoga Sutras of Patanjali (for serious yoginis!) by Sri S. Satchidananda

Wheresoever you go, go with all your heart.

—Confucius

SOURCES

Emerson, Ralph Waldo, and Oliver, Mary (editor). *The Essential Writings of Ralph Waldo Emerson* (Modern Library Paperback Classics). Modern Library, 2000.

Emerson, Ralph Waldo. *Ralph Waldo Emerson : Essays & Poems* (Library of America College Editions). Library of America, 1996.

Gandhi, Mahatma, and Fischer, Louis. *The Essential Gandhi : An Anthology of His Writings on His Life, Work, and Ideas* (Vintage Spiritual Classics). New York: Vintage, 2002.

Paltrow, Gwyneth. "Gwyneth gets buggy on 'Ellen'." *USA Today*, December, 2003.

Steinem, Gloria. *Revolution from Within*. Boston: Little, Brown, 1992.

Von Goethe, Johann Wolfgang, and Stopp, Elisabeth, and Hutchinson, Peter. *Goethe: Maxims and Reflections* (Penguin Classics). Penguin Books, 1999.

Whitman, Walt. *Leaves of Grass*. Philadelphia: David McKay, [c1900]; Bartleby.com, 1999. www.bartleby.com/142/. [Date of Printout].

Whitman, Walt. *Walt Whitman: Poetry and Prose*. Library of America, 1982.

Reference Material

Easwaran, Eknath (translator). *The Upanishads*. Nilgiri Press and the Blue Mountain Center of Meditation, 1987.

Feuerstein, Georg, Ph.D. *The Shambhala Encyclopedia of Yoga*. Boston & London: Shambhala, 2000.

Myss, Caroline, Ph.D. *Anatomy of the Spirit*. New York: Three Rivers Press, 1996.